MANAGEMENT?

Prentice Hall
FINANCIAL TIMES

In an increasingly competitive world, we believe it's quality of thinking that gives you the edge – an idea that opens new doors, a technique that solves a problem, or an insight that simply makes sense of it all. The more you know, the smarter and faster you can go.

That's why we work with the best minds in business and finance to bring cutting-edge thinking and best learning practice to a global market.

Under a range of leading imprints, including *Financial Times Prentice Hall*, we create world-class print publications and electronic products bringing our readers knowledge, skills and understanding, which can be applied whether studying or at work.

To find out more about Pearson Education publications, or tell us about the books you'd like to find, you can visit us at **www.pearsoned.co.uk**

PEARSON
Education

MANAGEMENT?
IT'S NOT WHAT YOU THINK!

HENRY MINTZBERG, BRUCE AHLSTRAND AND JOSEPH LAMPEL

Financial Times
Prentice Hall
is an imprint of

Harlow, England • London • New York • Boston • San Francisco • Toronto • Sydney • Singapore • Hong Kong
Tokyo • Seoul • Taipei • New Delhi • Cape Town • Madrid • Mexico City • Amsterdam • Munich • Paris • Milan

PEARSON EDUCATION LIMITED

Edinburgh Gate
Harlow CM20 2JE
Tel: +44 (0)1279 623623
Fax: +44 (0)1279 431059
Website: www.pearsoned.co.uk

First published in Great Britain in 2010

ISBN: 978-0-273-71967-0

British Library Cataloguing-in-Publication Data
A catalogue record for this book is available from the British Library

Library of Congress Cataloging-in-Publication Data
Mintzberg, Henry.
    Management : it's not what you think! / Henry Mintzberg, Bruce Ahlstrand and Joseph Lampel. -- 1st ed.
    ISBN 978-0-273-71967-0 (pbk.)
    1. Management. 2. Decision making. 3. Leadership. I. Lampel, Joseph. II. Ahlstrand, Bruce W. III. Title.
    HD31.M4566 2010
    658--dc22   2010018254

ARP Impression 98

Typeset in Classical Garamond 10/13pt by 30.
Printed in Great Britain by Clays Ltd, St Ives plc

CONTENTS

CHAPTER 4
MYTHS OF MANAGING

CHAPTER 5
MAXIMS OF MANAGING

CHAPTER 6
MASTERS OF MANAGING?

CHAPTER 7
METAMORPHOSING MANAGEMENT

PUBLISHER'S ACKNOWLEDGEMENTS

We are grateful to the following for permission to reproduce copyright material:

Figures

Figures on page 31 reprinted by permission, Edward R. Tufte, *The Cognitive Style of PowerPoint* (Graphics Press, Cheshire, CT, 2003), as appeared in *Wired* magazine, September 2003.

Text

Extract on page 5 this extract was published in *The Practice of Management*, Drucker, P., originally pub. 1954, 2nd revised edition 2007, Copyright Elsevier 2007; Extracts on pages 6–7, pages 7–10, pages 12–15 from *Managing*, Financial Times/Prentice Hall (Mintzberg, H. 2009) © Henry Mintzberg 2009, with permission from Henry Mintzberg Ltd; Extract on pages 9–12 from Decision Making: It's Not What You Think, *MIT Sloan Management Review*, Spring, pp. 89–93 (Mintzberg, H. and Westley, F. 2001), © 2010 by Massachusetts Institute of Technology. All rights reserved. Distributed by Tribune Media Services; Extract on pages 18–21 from Management and Magic, *California Management Review*, Vol. 27, No. 3, pp. 91–96 (Gimpl, M. L. and Dakin, S. R. 1984), Copyright © 1984, by the Regents of the University of California. Reprinted from the *California Management Review*, Vol. 27, No. 3. By permission of The Regents; Extract on pages 29–32 reprinted by permission, Edward R. Tufte, *The Cognitive Style of PowerPoint* (Graphics Press, Cheshire, CT, 2003), as appeared in *Wired* magazine, September 2003; Extract on pages 32-33 adapted with the permission of The Free Press, a Division of Simon & Schuster, Inc., from *The Rise and Fall of Strategic Planning* by Henry Mintzberg. Copyright © 1994 by Henry Mintzberg. All rights reserved and with permission from Pearson Education Ltd; Extract on pages 35–36 from 'WORDS' (a column), *Saturday Magazine, The Toronto Star*, 25/02/1989, p. M2 (Gloin, L.), reprinted with permission – Torstar Syndication Services; Epigraph on page 37 from *Dilbert and the Way of the Weasel* by Scott Adams. Copyright © 2002 by United Media, Inc. Reprinted by permission of HarperCollins Publishers and Knight Features Limited; Extract on pages 41–44 from Whole Foods CEO John

Mackey talks with Kai Ryssdal, transcript from 'Conversations from the Corner Office: John Mackey' from American Public Media's Marketplace®, © (p) 2007 American Public Media. Used with permission. All rights reserved; Extracts on pages 46–47, pages 87–90 from *Managers not MBAs*, Financial Times/Prentice Hall (Mintzberg, H. 2004), Pearson Education Ltd. and with permission from Henry Mintzberg Ltd; Extract on pages 47–48 from A descent in the dark by R. R. Reno, reprinted from *Commentary*, November 2008, by permission; copyright © 2008 by Commentary, Inc; Extract on pages 48–51 reprinted by permission of *Harvard Business Review*. From Enough Leadership by Henry Mintzberg, November 2004. Copyright © 2004 by the Harvard Business School Publishing Corporation; all rights reserved; Extract on pages 55–58 reprinted by permission of *Harvard Business Review*. From Spotting Management Fads by Danny Miller and Jon Hartwick, 1 October 2002. Copyright © 2002 by the Harvard Business School Publishing Corporation; all rights reserved; Extract on pages 58–65 reprinted by permission of Harvard Business Review. Adapted from Musings on Management by Henry Mintzberg, July–August 1996. Copyright © 1996 by the Harvard Business School Publishing Corporation; all rights reserved; Box on pages 65–67 adapted with the permission of The Free Press, a Division of Simon & Schuster, Inc., from *The Rise and Fall of Strategic Planning* by Henry Mintzberg. Copyright © 1994 by Henry Mintzberg. All rights reserved and with permission from Pearson Education Ltd; Extract on pages 67–69 adapted with the permission of The Free Press, a Division of Simon & Schuster, Inc., from *Forecasting, Planning and Strategy in the 21st Century* by Spyros G. Makridakis. Copyright © 1990 by Spyros G. Makridakis. All rights reserved; Extract on page 70 © Ashleigh Brilliant. www.ashleighbrilliant.com; Extract on pages 75–77 from *Parkinson's Law: The Pursuit of Progress* by C. Northcote Parkinson reproduced by permission of John Murray (Publishers) Limited; Extract on pages 77–81 from Maxims in Need of a Makeover by Justin Ewers [Money/Business] March 19, 2006, http://www.usnews.com/, Copyright 2006 U.S. News & World Report, L. P. Reprinted with permission; Epigraph on page 83 from Shepheard, Paul., *What Is Architecture? An Essay on Landscapes, Buildings, and Machines*, pp. quote from page 145, © 1994 Massachusetts Institute of Technology, by permission of The MIT Press; Extract on pages 91–94 from If his fellow Harvard MBAs are so clever, how come so many are now in disgrace?, *The Sunday Times*, 01/03/2009 (Philip Devies Broughton), © The Times March 1, 2009/nisyndication.com; Extract on page 103 adapted by Jim Clemmer from his book *Pathways to Performance* and published at www.JimClemmer.com; Extract on page 100 from When it comes to real change, too much objectivity may be fatal to the process, *Strategy and Leadership*, Vol. 25, Issue 2, March/April, pp. 6–12 (Hurst, D. K. 1997), © Emerald Group Publishing Limited all rights reserved; Extract on pages 101–104 from Perspectives on Strategy: The Real Story Behind

INTRODUCTION

MANAGEMENT? THINK AGAIN

Management: is it what you think it is? And is it only about thinking?

Frederick Taylor gave us time studies a century ago; strategic planning came along a half-century later. Both have left us with the impression that management is all about thinking – systematic thinking. Well, think again, about the art and craft of managing – the seeing and the feeling and the doing, beyond the thinking and the analysing and the planning.

This is the intention of this book: to get us all thinking again, opening up perspectives on this fascinating business of management, for managers themselves, those who work with managers, and anyone who aspires to join their ranks.

We do this through all sorts of pithy and provocative pieces. Some will make you laugh, others may make you cry (for poor old management itself). Some will seem wacky, irrelevant, irreverent – good, they are meant to be unsettling, sometimes even to make you angry, so that the irrelevant becomes relevant and the irreverent can sometimes be revered. We'd like you to see and to feel and to do management as you have not before.

Alongside articles from newspapers and excerpts from books and journals, you will find quotes and poems, outbursts, letters and Web things. We have put in whatever we could find that feels interesting, provocative and above all insightful.

For convenience and coherence, we have clustered all this into chapters. These make a little sense, but you needn't take them too seriously. Read as you wish, jump around (just as do so many managers) and skip what you care to ignore (unlike successful managers).

The first chapter is a 'management mosaic', meant to unfreeze you a little about what you think management is and what you think managers do – especially if you are a manager. Then we muse in Chapter 2 on the 'management of meaning', about how words are used and misused to represent the practice of managing.

Then it's on to leadership. These days, how can any book about management not leap into leadership? But beware: this chapter is called

'Misleading management'. You just might discover that leadership, too, is not what you think.

Myths abound in management, so Chapter 4 gets into these – fads, clichés, metaphors and more. Maxims, too, abound in management, so Chapter 5 presents lots of these, and what's wrong with them – including some maxims about such maxims.

Look left or right these days and there you will likely see an MBA (or maybe just look in a mirror). So we consider these masters of managing in Chapter 6. If you happen to be the one in the mirror, cover your eyes.

We live in times of great change. Have you heard that before? Not as in Chapter 7. Called 'Metamorphosing management', it might just change how you think about change.

To close the book on how to carry all this positively forward, Chapter 8 suggests various ways to manage modestly. Time to think about how to take management well beyond thinking.

This is the course in advanced physics. That means the instructor finds the subject confusing. If he didn't, the course would be called elementary physics. Luis Alvarez, Nobel Laureate.

CHAPTER 1
MANAGEMENT MOSAIC

If you always do what you always did, you will always get what you always got. [Anon]

Time for a little unfreezing: breaking down what we all 'know' about management. So we began with a mosaic of irreverent thoughts about management.

First comes the manager as orchestra conductor. We all know about this grand metaphor. Peter Drucker provides the first words. Well, read on, as Sune Carlson and then Leonard Sayles provide some other words. Management – you had better think again.

Next comes a cluster of short items, mostly from co-author Henry Mintzberg. The first is a list of words that have been used for managers over the ages, and most of them still. Managers: they're everyone you think. Then comes a list of all the qualities needed to be a successful manager. Superman would be found wanting. Management: it's everything you think. So the discussion turns to 'the inevitably flawed manager'. Then we move on to decision-making, to discover that it's not just what you think; it's also what you see and what you do. And last is a discussion from Henry's new book about the dynamics of managing. In this job, how can anyone possibly think?

In case you miss the point, there follows a classic piece by Albert Shapero, who contrasts the image of contemporary MANAGEMENT (his capitals) – staff-driven, bureaucratic, competitive, impersonal – with managing tuned to 'the natural messiness of life'.

As if all this is not problem enough, we close with an article by Gimpl and Dakin called 'Management and magic'. It offers some surprising thoughts about this supposedly rational job: they link planning to superstitious behaviour, forecasting to magic, and control to the illusion of control. Take special note of the quote that closes this chapter.

THE MANAGER AS ORCHESTRA CONDUCTOR
BY PETER DRUCKER, SUNE CARLSON AND LEONARD SAYLES

One analogy [for the manager] is the conductor of a symphony orchestra, through whose effort, vision and leadership, individual instrumental parts that are so much noise by themselves, become the living whole of music. But the conductor has the composer's score: he is only interpreter. The manager is both composer and conductor.

PETER DRUCKER, *THE PRACTICE OF MANAGEMENT*, HARPER & ROW PUBLISHERS, 1954, PP. 341–342.

Before we made the study, I always thought of a chief executive as the conductor of an orchestra, standing aloof on his platform. Now I am in some respect inclined to see him as the puppet in the puppet-show with hundreds of people pulling the strings and forcing him to act in one way or another.

SUNE CARLSON, *EXECUTIVE BEHAVIOUR*, STROMBERG, 1951, P. 52.

The manager is like a symphony orchestra conductor, endeavoring to maintain a melodious performance in which the contributions of the various instruments are coordinated and sequenced, patterned and paced, while the orchestra members are having various personal difficulties, stage hands are moving music stands, alternating excessive heat and cold are creating audience and instrumental problems, and the sponsor of the concert is insisting on irrational changes in the program.

LEONARD SAYLES, *ADMINISTRATION IN COMPLEX ORGANIZATIONS*, MCGRAW-HILL, 1964, P. 6.

MANAGEMENT: BE CAREFUL WHAT YOU THINK
BY HENRY MINTZBERG

Managers: they're everyone you think

President
Prime Minister
Middle Manager
Administrator
Official
Foreman
Steward
Boss
Head Honcho
Conductor
Superior
Chief
Kingpin
Potentate
Lord
Pharaoh
Caesar
Emperor
King
Shogun
Czar
Maharaja
Headmistress
Head
Sheik
Sultan
Fuhrer
Viceroy
Superintendent
Director
Executive
Dictator
Oligarch
CEO
COO
CFO
CLO

Source: Adapted from Henry Mintzberg, *Managing*, FT/Prentice Hall, 2009.

Management: It's Everything you think

Lists of the qualities of effective managers and leaders abound. They are usually short – who would take dozens of items seriously? For example, in a brochure to promote its EMBA program, entitled 'What makes a leader?', the University of Toronto Business School answered: 'The courage to challenge the status quo. To flourish in a demanding environment. To collaborate for the greater good. To set clear direction in a rapidly changing world. To be fearlessly decisive' (Rotman School, circa 2005).

The trouble is that these lists are not consistent – they contain all sorts of different characteristics. For example, where is native intelligence on the list above, or being a good listener, or just plain having energy? Surely these are important too. No problem: they appear on other lists. So if we are to find out what makes a manager truly effective, we shall have to combine all the lists.

This, for the sake of a better world, has been done in Table 1. It lists the qualities from the various lists that I have found, with a few missing favorites of my own added in. This list contains 52 items. Be all 52 and you are bound to be an effective manager. Even if not a human one.

If you want to uncover someone's flaws, marry them or else work for them

The inevitably flawed manager

All of this is part of our 'romance of leadership' (Meindl *et al.*, 1985), that on one hand puts ordinary mortals on managerial pedestals ('Rudolph is the perfect manager for this job – he will save us'), and on the other hand allows us to vilify them as they come crashing down ('How could Rudolph have failed us so?'). Yet some managers do stay up, if not on that silly pedestal. How so?

The answer is simple: they are flawed – we are all flawed – but their particular flaws are not fatal, at least under the circumstances. (Superman, you might recall, was flawed too – remember Kryptonite?)

If you want to uncover someone's flaws, marry them or else work for them. Their flaws will quickly become apparent. So too will something else, at least if you are a mature human being who made a reasonably good choice: that you can usually live with those flaws. Managers and marriages do succeed. The world, as a consequence, continues to unfold in its inimitably imperfect way.[1]

This, of course, means that those superman lists of leadership qualities are also flawed: people often succeed even while failing on some of these qualities. But more to the point, these lists are often wrong. For example, leaders should be decisive, and they should be decent: who can argue with that? For starters, anyone who has worked for an indecent leader who got results. And how about Americans whose president learned the importance of

Table 1 Composite list of basic qualities for assured managerial effectiveness

courageous	energetic/enthusiastic
committed	upbeat/optimistic
curious	ambitious
confident	tenacious/ persistent
candid	zealous
	collaborative/participative/cooperative
reflective	*engaging*
insightful	supportive/sympathetic/empathetic
open-minded/tolerant (of people,	stable
ambiguities and ideas)	dependable
innovative	fair
communicative (including being a good	accountable
listener)	ethical/honest
connected/informed	consistent
perceptive	flexible
	balanced
	integrative
thoughtful/intelligent/wise	
analytic/objective	
pragmatic	
decisive (action-oriented)	
pro-active	
charismatic	
passionate	
inspiring	
visionary	tall*

Compiled from various sources; my own favorites in italics.

* This item appeared on no list that I saw. But it might rank ahead of many of the other items because studies have shown that managers are on average taller than other people. To quote from a 1920 study, entitled *The Executive and his Control of Men*, based on research done a lot more carefully than much of what we find in the great journals of today, Enoch Burton Gowin addressed the question: 'Viewing it as a chemical machine, is a larger body able to supply a greater amount of energy?' More specifically, might there be 'some connection between an executive's physique, as measured by height and weight, and the importance of the position he holds?' (1920: 22, 31). The answer, in statistic after statistic gathered by the author, is yes. Bishops, for example, averaged greater height than the preachers of small towns; superintendents of school systems were taller than principals of schools. Other data on railroad executives, governors, etc. supported these findings. The 'Superintendents of Street Cleaning' were actually the second tallest of all, after the 'Reformers.' (The 'Socialist Organizers' were just behind the 'police chiefs', but well up there.) Musicians were at the bottom of the list (p. 25).

being decisive in a case study classroom at Harvard and certainly was decisive in his decision to go to war with Iraq. The University of Toronto list calls this quality 'fearlessly decisive'. He sure was.

As for some of the other items on the University of Toronto list, that president's arch enemy in Afghanistan certainly 'had the courage to challenge the status quo', while Ingvar Kamprad, who built IKEA into one of the most successful retail chains ever, reportedly took fifteen years to 'set [its] clear direction in a changing world'. Actually he succeeded because the furniture world was not changing: *he* changed it.

Reference

Meindl, J. R., Ehrlich, S. B. and Dukerich, J. M. (1985) 'The romance of leadership', *Administrative Sciences Quarterly*, 30, 78–102.

Footnotes

1 Not always. Politicians seem to have become particularly adept at hiding flaws until they become fatal. For example, the object of the political debates on television is to demonstrate that your opponent is flawed while you are not (or at least not revealed until you are elected). The assumption is that the flawed candidate should lose. Perhaps this theatrical farce is one reason why people these days are so fed up with political leadership.

Source: Excerpted from Henry Mintzberg, *Managing*, FT/Prentice Hall, 2009.

Decision Making: It's not what you think
with Frances Westley

How should decisions be made? Easy, we figured that out long ago. First define the problem, then diagnose its causes, next design possible solutions, and finally decide which is best. And, of course, implement the choice.

But do people always make decisions that way? We propose that this rational, or 'thinking first', model of decision making should be supplemented with two very different models – a 'seeing first' and a 'doing first' model.

Consider how a real decision was made, a personal one in this case. It begins with a call from an aunt.

'Hi, kiddo. I want to buy you a housewarming present. What's the color scheme in your new apartment?'

'Color scheme? Betty, you've got to be kidding. I'll have to ask Lisa. Lisa, Betty wants to know the color scheme of the apartment.'

'Black,' daughter Lisa says.

'Black? Lisa, I've got to live there.'

'Black,' she repeats.

A few days later, father and daughter find themselves in a furniture store. They try every desk, every chair: Nothing works. Shopper's lethargy sets in. Then Lisa spots a black stool: 'Wouldn't that look great against the white counter?' And they're off. Within an hour, they have picked out everything – in black, white and steel gray.

The extraordinary thing about this ordinary story is that our conventional theories of decision making can't explain it. It is not even clear what the final decision was: to buy the stool; to get on with furnishing an apartment; to do so in black and white; to create a new lifestyle? Decision making can be mysterious.

The limits of 'thinking first'

Rational decision making has a clearly identified process: define → diagnose → design → decide. However, the rational approach turns out to be uncommon.

Years ago, one of us studied a host of decisions, delineating the steps and then laying them out. A decision process for building a new plant was typical. The process kept cycling back, interrupted by new events, diverted by opportunities and so on, going round and round until finally a solution emerged. The final action was as clear as a wave breaking on the shore, but explaining how it came to be is as hard as tracing the origin of that wave back into the ocean.

Often decisions do not so much emerge as erupt. Here is how Alexander Kotov, the chess master, has described a sudden insight that followed lengthy analysis:

'So, I mustn't move the knight. Try the rook move again. . . . At this point you glance at the clock. "My goodness! Already 30 minutes gone on thinking about whether to move the rook or the knight. If it goes on like this you'll really be in time trouble." And then suddenly you are struck by the happy idea – why move rook or knight? What about B–QN1? And without any more ado, without analysis at all, you move the bishop. Just like that.'

Perhaps, then, decision making means periods of groping followed by sudden sharp insights that lead to crystallization. Or perhaps it is a form of 'organized anarchy', as Stanford professor James March and colleagues have written. They characterize decision making as 'collections of choices looking for problems, issues and feelings looking for decision situations in which they may be aired, solutions looking for issues to which they might be an answer, and decision makers looking for work.'

Maybe messy, real-life decision making makes more sense than we think

But is the confusion in the process, as described by those authors, or is it confusion in the observers? Maybe messy, real-life decision making makes more sense than we think, precisely because so much of it is beyond conscious thought.

'Seeing first'

Insight – 'seeing into' – suggests that decisions, or at least actions, may be driven as much by what is seen as by what is thought. As Mozart said, the best part about creating a symphony was being able to 'see the whole of it at a single glance in my mind'. So, understanding can be visual as well as conceptual.

In W. Koehler's well-known 1920s experiment, an ape struggled to reach a banana placed high in its cage. Then it *saw* the box in the corner – not just noticed it, but realized what could be done with it – and its problem was solved. Likewise, after Alexander Fleming really *saw* the mold that had killed the bacteria in some of his research samples (in other words, when he realized how that mold could be used), he and his colleague were able to give us penicillin. The same can be true for strategic vision. Vision requires the courage to see what others do not – and that means having both the confidence and the experience to recognize the sudden insight for what it is.

A theory in Gestalt psychology developed by G. Wallas in the 1920s identifies four steps in creative discovery: preparation → incubation → illumination → verification.

Preparation must come first. As Louis Pasteur put it, 'Chance favors only the prepared mind.' Deep knowledge, usually developed over years, is followed by incubation, during which the unconscious mind mulls over the issue. Then with luck (as with Archimedes in the bathtub), there is that flash of illumination. That eureka moment often comes after sleep – because in sleep, rational thinking is turned off, and the unconscious has greater freedom. The conscious mind returns later to make the logical argument: verification (reasoning it all out in linear order for purposes of elaboration and proof). But that takes time. There is a story of a mathematician who solved a formula in his sleep. Holding it in his mind's eye, he was in no rush to write it down. When he did, it took him four months!

Great insights may be rare, but what industry cannot trace its origins to one or more of them? Moreover, little insights occur to all of us all the time. No one should accept any theory of decision making that ignores insight.

'Doing first'

But what happens when you don't see it and can't think it up? Just do it. That is how pragmatic people function when stymied: They get on with it, believing that if they do 'something', the necessary thinking could follow. It's experimentation – trying something so that you can learn.

A theory for 'doing first', popularized by Karl Weick, goes like this: enactment → selection → retention.

That means doing various things, finding out which among them works, making sense of that and repeating the successful behaviors while discarding the rest. Successful people know that when they are stuck, they must experiment. Thinking may drive doing, but doing just as surely drives thinking. We don't just think in order to act, we also act in order to think.

Show us almost any company that has diversified successfully, and we will show you a company that has learned by doing, one whose diversification strategy emerged through experience. Such a company at the outset may have laid out a tidy strategy on the basis of assessing its weaknesses and strengths (or, if after 1990, its 'core competencies'), which it almost certainly got

'Thinking first' features the qualities of	*'Seeing first' features the qualities of*	*'Doing first' features the qualities of*
Science	Art	Craft
Planning, programming	Visioning, imagining	Venturing, learning
The verbal	The visual	The visceral
Facts	Ideas	Experiences

wrong. How can you tell a strength from a weakness when you are entering a new sphere? You have no choice but to try things out. Then you can identify the competencies that really matter. Action is important; if you insist on 'thinking first' and, for example, doing formalized strategic planning (which is really part of the same thing), you may in fact discourage learning . . .

So how did you choose your mate? Did you think first: specify all the criteria, then list all the alternatives and finally choose one or was it love at first sight? Maybe you acted first – we'll let you think about that, and its consequences.

Source: MIT *Sloan Management Review*, Spring 2001. © 2010 by Massachusetts Institute of Technology. All rights reserved. Distributed by Tribune Media Services.

Managing: How can you possibly think?

Have a look at the popular images of managing – the conductor on the podium, those executives sitting at desks in *New Yorker* cartoons – and you get one impression of the job: well ordered, carefully controlled. Watch some managers at work and you will likely find something far different: a hectic pace, lots of interruptions, more responding than initiating. So let's have a good look at some of these facts, compared with that folklore.

Folklore: The manager is a reflective, systematic planner. We have this common image of the manager, especially in a senior job, sitting at a desk thinking great thoughts, making grand decisions, and above all systematically planning out the future. There is a good deal of evidence about this, but not a shred of it supports this image.

Facts: Study after study has shown that (a) managers work at an unrelenting pace, (b) their activities are typically characterized by brevity, variety, fragmentation and interruption, and (c) they are strongly oriented to action.

(a) The Pace Reports on the hectic pace of managerial work have been consistent, from foreman to chief executives. As one CEO put it, the work of managing is 'one damn thing after another'. Managing is an open-ended job with a perpetual preoccupation: the manager can never be free to forget the work, never having the pleasure of knowing, even temporarily, that there is nothing left to do.

(b) The Brevity, Variety, Fragmentation, and Interruption Most work in society involves specialization and concentration. Engineers and programmers can spend months designing a machine or developing some software. Managers can expect no such concentration of efforts. Their work is fragmented and loaded with interruptions. Why? Because they don't wish to discourage the flow of current information, also because they develop a sensitive appreciation for the *opportunity cost* of their own time: no matter what they are doing, managers are plagued by what they might do and what they *must* do.

(c) The Action Managers like action – activities that move, change, flow, are tangible, current, non-routine. Don't expect to find much general planning or open-ended touring in this job; look instead for tangible delving into specific concerns. Does this mean that managers don't plan? Sure they plan; we all plan. But the real planning of the organization, at least in a strategic sense, takes place significantly in the heads of its managers and implicitly in the context of their daily actions, not in some abstract process reserved for a mountain retreat or a bunch of forms to fill out.

Folklore: The manager depends on aggregated information, best supplied by a formal system. In keeping with the classical image of the manager perched on some sort of hierarchical pedestal, managers are supposed to receive their important information from some sort of comprehensive, formalized Management Information System. But this has never proved true, not before computers, not after they appeared, not even in these days of the internet.

Fact: Managers tend to favor the informal media of communication, especially the oral ones of telephone calls and meetings, also the electronic one of email. Studies have found managing to be between 60 to 90% oral. The manager does not leave the telephone, the meeting, or the email to get back to work. These contacts *are* the work. As Jeanne Liedtka of the Darden School has put it: 'Talk is the technology of leadership.' Moreover gossip, hearsay, and speculation form a good part of the manager's information diet. Why? Because today's gossip can become tomorrow's fact. But then it may be too late: manager's have to know sooner, not later.

Formal information is firm, definitive – at the limit, it comprises hard numbers and clear reports. But informal information can be much richer, even if less reliable. On the telephone, there is tone of voice and the chance to interact; in meetings, there is also facial expressions, gestures and other body language. As a consequence of all this, the strategic data banks of organizations remain at least as much in the heads of their managers as in the files of their computers.

Folklore: Managing is mostly about hierarchical relationships between a 'superior' and 'subordinates'. Our use of these awful labels should be telling us something.

Fact: Managing is as much about lateral relationships among colleagues and associates. Study after study has shown that managers, at all levels, spend a great deal of their contact time – often close to half or more – with a wide variety of people external to their own units: customers, suppliers, partners, government and trade officials, other stakeholders, as well as all kinds of colleagues in their own organization. We might thus characterize the manager's position as the neck of an hourglass, sitting between a network of outside contacts and the internal unit being managed.

Folklore: Managers maintain tight control – of their time, their activities, their units. The orchestra conductor standing on the platform waving the baton has been a popular metaphor for managing. Much of it is pure myth.

Fact: The manager is neither conductor nor puppet: control in this job tends to be covert more than overt. If managerial work is like orchestra conducting, then it is not the grand image of performance, where everything has been well rehearsed and everyone is on his or her best behavior, the audience included. It is rehearsal, where all sorts of things can go wrong and must be corrected quickly.

Managers exercise control despite the constraints, by using two degrees of freedom in particular. They make a set of initial decisions that define many of their subsequent commitments (for example, to start a project that, once underway, demands their time). And they adapt to their own ends activities in which they *must* engage (for example, by using a ceremonial occasion to lobby on behalf of their organization). Thus the effective managers seem to be, not those with the greatest degrees of freedom, but the ones who use to advantage whatever degrees of freedom they can find.

The impact of the internet

How has the internet, especially email, influenced all this? Has it changed managing fundamentally? No and maybe yes.

This powerful new medium has vastly increased the speed, range, and volume of communication. Yet like conventional mail, it is restricted by the poverty of words alone: there is no tone of voice to hear, no gestures to see, no presence to feel, usually no images to see. It can give the impression of being in touch while the only thing actually being touched is the keyboard.

The internet may be driving much management practice over the edge, making it so frenetic that it becomes dysfunctional

Perhaps most significantly, email increases the pace and pressure of managing, and often the interruptions as well. Beyond the enticement of 'You've got mail!' add a BlackBerry in the pocket – the tether to the global village – and you've got interruptions galore.

Does the internet enhance or diminish the control managers have over their own work? Obviously it depends on the manager. As with most technologies, the internet can be used for better or for worse. You can be mesmerized by it, and so let it manage you. Or you can understand its power as well as its dangers, and so manage it.

Think of the power of email to connect, the power of internet to access and transmit information. Think too of the pressures and pace of managerial work, the needs to respond, the nagging feeling of being out of control.

Might the internet, by giving the illusion of control, in fact be robbing managers of control? One conclusion seems evident: the internet is not changing the practice of management fundamentally, but rather reinforcing characteristics that we have been seeing for decades. In other words, the changes are in the same direction, of degree, not kind.

But the devil can be in the detail. Changes of degree can have profound effects, amounting to changes of kind. The internet may be driving much management practice over the edge, making it so frenetic that it becomes dysfunctional: too superficial, too disconnected, too conformist. Perhaps the ultimately connected manager has become disconnected from what matters, while the freneticness is destroying the practice of managing itself.

Source: Excerpted from Chapter 2 of Henry Mintzberg, *Managing*, Berrett Koehler and FTPN, 2010.

WHAT MANAGEMENT SAYS AND WHAT MANAGERS DO
BY ALBERT SHAPERO

Of the existing literature on management, 95 percent is American, and most of the rest is paraphrased or lifted from the American literature. Leading the field in prestige and circulation (160,000) is *Harvard Business Review*. Like the school from which it issues, *H. B. R.* is a major fount of MANAGEMENT, as distinguished from management. Management is what managers do. MANAGEMENT is a view of what managers do at major corporations – a view shared by business schools, management consultants, and many business and management journals.

Accordingly, the appearance of *On Management* (Harper & Row, $17.95), articles selected from twenty-five years of *H. B. R.*, is an event of some importance. The book should be considered not only in terms of its contents (which are undated to emphasize their timelessness), but also in terms of the opportunity it affords us to examine MANAGEMENT, its relevance to real-life management, and its profound influence upon the way we work and live.

Images of control, pictures of chaos

For whom is MANAGEMENT; to whom is it addressed? It is certainly not for all of the 13 million or so business enterprises in the U. S. To cite one piece of evidence, only a single article in *On Management* is directed to 'smaller' companies and speaks in terms of what top executives should do in the absence of operations research, planning departments, and large-scale computer capacity.

MANAGEMENT, it appears, is for the FORTUNE 500 and perhaps 2,000 more of the world's largest companies. But there remains a question whether even for these large enterprises MANAGEMENT relates to the actualities of corporate managerial life. The term MANAGEMENT conjures up images of control, rationality, systematics; but studies of what managers actually do depict behaviors and situations that are chaotic, unplanned, and charged with improvisation.

Reports on what managers do, made over the past thirty years in various countries and industries, are all amazingly similar in the pictures they paint of corporate managerial life: the fifty-five-to-sixty-hour week; the lists of things to do that never get past the first item; 40 to 60 percent of their time spent in meetings, 90 percent of which were called by others; 15 percent of their time on the phone; an average of fifteen to thirty minutes between interruptions; stolen half-days to produce required reports.

The managerial life at every level is reflexive – responding to calls, memos, personnel problems, fire drills, budget meetings, and personnel reviews. The manager's days are controlled by other people. I have asked hundreds of managers how much of their time is spent in such reflective activities as planning, thinking, or analyzing. They consistently say between 5 and 10 percent – and then admit to lying.

The manager's days are controlled by other people

Occasionally, however, we find at managerial levels individuals who go twenty-four hours without being interrupted by meetings or phone calls. They are the long-range planners, the people in O. R., E. D. P., financial or market planning, or market research. MANAGEMENT is really for them. The bulk of the articles in *On Management* are concerned with ideas from the world of the staff functionary. These articles are either directed to the interests of the staff person in terms of analytical how-to's, or they tell the chief executive to think like a staff person, support and take part in staff activities, or else.

The size of staffs and the influence of staffs on the conduct of business and government have grown very considerably over the past several decades. In 1920 nonproduction workers made up 19 percent of the manufacturing work force. Today about 27 percent of the manufacturing work force is not directly involved in production. The large and growing number of people not occupied with the apparent central business of their companies should give us pause.

Even more worrisome, however, is the increasing general preoccupation with the analytics that are the domain of staff people. Staff people are committed to the products of the analytics, such as models, graphs, ratios, printouts, and not to the people and things they represent. With very exceptional exceptions the staff person has seldom spent more than token time on-line in producing, selling, or servicing the products of a company.

Analysis in Wonderland

The staff view of life is the very essence of MANAGEMENT, and that is the view nurtured by our better business schools. Selling and manufacturing have been virtually expunged from the curriculum, and in their place we have analytical surrogates such as consumer behavior, market research, operations research, financial analysis, organization theory, and accounting theory. These are intellectually satisfying pursuits, but they are not directly involved with the realities, joys, and difficulties of real operations.

Twenty-five years of MANAGEMENT have resulted in an Analysis in Wonderland outlook where abstractions are reality and where people and things are ciphers of difficulties to be dealt with. In the MANAGEMENT world view, a typical managerial task is using E. D. P. with an M. I. S. to measure R. O. I. so the C. E. O. can please the board of directors with projected results of corporate competitive strategy as depicted in the L. R. P. graphics.

Traditionally, the staff person lived a life of frustration and petulance, trying to influence men of power who came out of production or sales. The constant effort was to get 'them' to listen. The successful staff person was a vizier, a gray eminence, turned to by the boss, wielding power through legitimate managers. With the growth of MANAGEMENT, however, the man of power is increasingly taking on a staff outlook.

The effects of twenty-five years of MANAGEMENT are manifest and troublesome. A 1975 issue of *Harvard Business Review* shows that corporations with assets exceeding $10 million have been outperformed by smaller companies over the past several years in terms of return on stockholders' equity. U. S. corporate productivity is being outdone by Europeans to whom, under various technical-assistance programs, we promulgated our pre-MANAGEMENT methods of production and selling.

The effects of twenty-five years of MANAGEMENT are manifest and troublesome

The staff-driven, bureaucratic, competitive, impersonal climate generated by MANAGEMENT has had and continues to have disastrous effects on many aspects of our lives. The recent bribery revelations, for example, are no passing accident. They are inexorable results of abstraction from direct concern for workers and customers with names, and direct contact with processes and products that have substance.

Why not bribe officials if it will get you the sales and make the annual report look good? Why not lower product quality to just above the lawsuit level? Why provide more than the minimum of service required to maintain profits? You will swiftly be promoted to another department if you can keep the numbers right. Show me a thirty-five-year-old executive with an M. B. A. from a very good school who wants to stay in direct sales because he likes making customers happy, who likes his colleagues and wishes them every success, and who would never do anything unethical, and I will show you a man known as a religious type, as a 'loser'.

Making it work anyway

Eventually, the strange culture of MANAGEMENT will retreat. It has been able to prevail to the extent it has only because, no matter how you design a system, real human beings will make it work anyway. The immense goodwill and natural capabilities of hundreds of thousands of managers are committed each day to making sense of the wide gap between MANAGEMENT and the chaotic realities of daily existence. With feelings of guilt and inadequacy in the face of the latest methods they are urged to use, they give MANAGEMENT lip service, and still produce and sell as required.

When we forswear MANAGEMENT, do we forgo rationality? Is this the lesson of the past twenty-five years? No! Never have we had more need of rationality, but the kind of rationality rooted in observed phenomena. We need to return to a rationality tuned to the natural messiness of life, and not one dedicated to neat abstractions. There are no straight lines in nature, and despite the linearities depicted by MANAGEMENT, there are no straight lines in management either.

Source: This article appeared in the May 1976 issue of *Fortune* magazine.

MANAGEMENT AND MAGIC
BY MARTIN I. GIMPL AND STEPHEN R. DAKIN

There is a fundamental paradox in human behavior – the more unpredictable the world becomes, the more we seek out and rely upon forecasts and predictions to determine what we should do. It is not unreasonable to draw an analogy between weather forecasting under conditions of extreme uncertainty, and management's continuing interest in forecasting and planning activities in a highly uncertain trading climate. Why do we continue to seek forecasts when the weather is unpredictable? It is our contention that management's enchantment with the magical rites of long-range planning, forecasting, and several other future-oriented techniques is a manifestation of anxiety-relieving superstitious behavior, and that forecasting and planning have the same function that magical rites have. Anthropologists and psychologists have long argued that magical rites and superstitious behavior serve very important functions: they make the world seem more deterministic and give us confidence in our ability to cope, they unite the managerial tribe, and they induce us to take action, at least when the omens are favorable (Perlmuter and Monty, 1977). In addition, these rites may act to preserve the status quo.

Superstitious behavior is behavior which in the eyes of a 'reasonable' man is unlikely to have the causal effect it is believed to have (Jahoda, 1970). E.J. Langer (1975) refers to this as 'illusion of control' – the belief that events are causally related when objectively they are not.

Superstitions increase in number and intensity as our environment becomes more uncomfortable and more unpredictable. Superstitions abound during periods of plague, famine, and warfare. B. Malinowski (1951), a social anthropologist, argued that 'man resorts to magic only where chance and circumstances are not fully controlled by knowledge'. To illustrate the point, he described the fishing practices of the Trobriand Archipelago. Those who are in villages in the inner lagoon, where fishing is easy and safe, do not have any magical procedures associated with it. By contrast, those in villages on the open sea, where obtaining fish is more hazardous and uncertain, have many superstitions concerning fishing.

When people feel out of control there is a tendency toward inactivity

Similarly, in today's uncertain trading climate we might expect a similar emergence of 'superstitious' behavior as managers try to predict and control events which, in terms of current conditions and technology, are manifestly unpredictable and out of control. Such conditions foster the use of predictive devices ranging from capital budgeting to assessment centers. Do these devices work? If not, then we may legitimately brand their continued use as superstition . . .

[S]uperstition often involves the emergence of cult-leaders, or 'witch-detectives', who may direct proceedings and interpret omens. Similarly, times of uncertainty in our modern world breed magicians, witch-detectives, and consultants. Why? As John Kenneth Galbraith (1982) says:

In an uncertain subject matter such as economics or psychiatry, there is something wonderfully compelling about those who are sure. Also, much discussion of money has a necromantic aspect; mystery, even witchcraft, is presumed to be involved. A special reputation accrues to those who, affirming the mystery, presume to penetrate it. They are in touch with the occult; others should trust them.

. . . Superstitions are the vehicle whereby charismatic leaders provide feelings of certainty in otherwise uncertain times. The existence of these leaders may boost confidence, guide action, and, if things continue to go wrong, provide a scapegoat for the sufferer. The difference between modern economic forecasters and the shaman predicting and inducing rain may be more in their appearance than in the substance of their predictions . . .

Implicit in the discussion so far has been the notion that superstitions are undesirable; that illusions of control should be discouraged. On the contrary, it is apparent that under certain circumstances superstitious behavior can be highly functional for both individuals and groups.

One function that may be overlooked is that, under conditions of extreme ambiguity, people may readily opt for helplessness (Perlmuter and Monty, 1977). When people feel out of control there is a tendency toward inactivity – to do nothing. Under such circumstances, of course, it is more appropriate to do something – anything – since activity may uncover elements of control which were previously unnoticed. Thus, to the extent that superstitions give the feeling of control they may encourage necessary activity.

A second major function is that in a random world the best course of action is random action. Well-designed magical rites do precisely this – they encourage random action . . .

O.K. Moore (1957) tells of the use of caribou bones among the Labrador Indians. When food is short because of poor hunting, the Indians consult an oracle to determine the direction the hunt should take. The shoulder blade of the caribou is put over the hot coals of a fire; cracks in the bones induced by the heat are then interpreted as a map. The directions indicated by this oracle are basically random. Moore points out that this is a highly efficacious method because if the Indians did not use a random number generator they would fall prey to their previous biases and tend to over-hunt certain areas. Furthermore, any regular pattern of the hunt would give the animals a chance to develop avoidance techniques. By randomizing their hunting patterns the Indians' chances of reaching game are enhanced . . .

There is an additional and secondary function that should be mentioned. While superstition is useful if it randomizes action, the magical rites associated with superstitions are useful in *justifying* random action. Devons has noted how difficult it is for government or nationalized industry to plan sensibly, and says:

> *No Chancellor of the Exchequer could introduce his proposals for monetary and fiscal policy in the House of Commons by saying, 'I have looked at all the forecasts, and some go one way, some another; so I decided to toss a coin and assume inflationary tendencies if it came down heads and deflationary if it came down tails.'*

Thus, magical rites, including the use of economic statistics, permit managers to justify taking random action.

Having said all this, it is clear that many managerial superstitions are *dys*functional. The basic reason for their dysfunctionality is that, while they reduce anxiety and build confidence in times of uncertainty, they may simply provide justification for continuing past practice rather than sanctioning innovation. Most techniques do not generate random data but introduce a biased series – the caribou are likely to pick up your pattern.

References

Devons, E. *Essays in Economics*, London: Allen and Unwin, 1961.

Galbraith, J.K. 'You can't argue with a monetarist', a feature article in *The Christchurch Press*, 23 September 1982; from the London Observer Service.

Jahoda, G. *The Psychology of Superstition*, New York: Pelican, 1970 p. 127.

Langer, E.J. 'The illusion of control', *Journal of Personality and Social Psychology*, 32, 1975, pp. 311–328.

Malinowski, B. *Magic, Science, Religion and Other Essays*, quoted in Romans, G.C., *The Human Group*, London: Routledge Kegan Paul, 1951 pp. 321–323.

Moore, O.K. 'Divination – a new perspective', *American Anthropologist*, 59, 1957, pp. 69–74.

Perlmuter, L.C. and Monty, R.A. 'The importance of perceived control: fact or fantasy?', *American Scientist*, 65, 1977, pp. 959–964.

Source: © 1984, by The Regents of the University of California. Reprinted from the *California Management Review*, 'Management and magic' by M.L. Gimpl and S.R. Dakin, Vol. 27, No. 3. By permission of the Regents.

If you're not confused, you don't know what's going on. Jack Welch (as CEO of General Electric)

CHAPTER 2
MANAGEMENT OF MEANING

We don't see things as they are. We see things as we are. [The Talmud]

Managing meaning – for better and for worse: this is the subject of Chapter 2.

Jargon is the hand-maiden of modern management. It provides assurance, confers membership, and beams out the message that 'we know what we are doing'. Smullyan fires the first shot by challenging one of the seemingly most neutral words of managing: 'problem-solving'. Maybe that's where the problems begin. Then along comes Lucy Kellaway with a machine-gun round of challenges: to a whole mother-load of 'waffle words' all crammed into one sentence by a consulting firm: Broad. Strategic. Focus. Highly integrated system. Capabilities. Fundamental. Strategies.

'Mana-gems' follow: wonderful typographical errors. Be prepared: there's a lot of wisdom in serendipity. (Anyone for a brief *executive?)*

How is most of today's jargon delivered? Might you have guessed: PowerPoint? Edward Tufte calls it evil, since it 'turns everything into a sales pitch'.

Henry Mintzberg follows this with a look at strategic planning as a public relations exercise – to impress those who wish to be thought of as modern and professional. Henry suggests that there are no winners in this: outsiders get useless pronouncements and junior managers waste their time filling out forms while the senior managers get distracted from important issues.

Then R. Farson looks at some of the contradictory components of communication. For example, he notes that the healthy organisation needs both full and accurate communication and distortion and deception. We end all of this with a reading on a 'buzz-word' generator. Now, you too can write impressive – 'sounding memos and reports that mean absolutely nothing'.

PROBLEMS, PROBLEMS, PROBLEMS
BY RAYMOND SMULLYAN

Once when I was playing for a musician, he complimented me on the way I played a particular passage. He told me how well I handled a certain modulation and added, 'You don't realize in what a remarkable way you have solved this problem!'

I must say, I was thunderstruck . . . I was totally unaware of any problem let alone solving one! The whole idea of 'problem solving', especially in music, strikes me as so weird. Not only weird, but most disharmonious and destructive. Is that how you think of life, as a series of problems to be solved? No wonder you don't enjoy living more than you do!

> *the moment one labels something as a 'problem' that's when the real problem starts*

To compliment a musician, or any other artist, on having 'solved problems' to me is absolutely analogous to complimenting the waves of the ocean for solving such a complex system of partial differential equations. Of course, the ocean does its 'waving' in accordance with these differential equations, but it hardly solves them … I believe my objection to the notion of 'problem' is due to my deep conviction that the moment one labels something as a 'problem' that's when the real problem starts.

Source: Raymond Smullyan

ACCENTURE'S NEXT CHAMPION OF WAFFLE WORDS
BY LUCY KELLAWAY

When one door closes, another one opens. On Thursday the prison gates clanked shut behind Martin Lukes in Florida but, in London, the door of an office inside Accenture swung ajar, revealing Mark Foster, a middle-aged white man with a long-winded title.

Just as I was putting my final full stop to the story of the jargon-talking executive, someone forwarded me an internal e-mail sent by Accenture's group chief executive for management consulting. Immediately I saw that this man could be a possible successor to Lukes. I don't know if Mr Foster has Martin's way with women or whether his golf swing is any good, as I have never met him. However, I have seen one of his e-mails and that is enough to convince me that, when it comes to world-class jargon, there is clear blue water between him and the rest – even at Accenture, where the bar, as they call it, is set so very high.

This isn't the first time I've singled out Accenture for its work in the jargon space. A couple of years ago, I wrote a column about its annual report, which was a perfect snapshot of the ugliest business language of the time. Inside was an orgy of 'relentless passion' and 'delivering value'. The point, presumably, was to impress clients.

Yet Mr Foster's e-mail is more troubling as it shows top people write like this even when they think no clients are looking. His memo was addressed to 'All Accenture Senior Executives' – though title inflation being what it is, this probably stretches to include the cleaner. Indeed as 'group chief executive', Mr Foster is in a band of eight others with the same commanding title, and still has a couple of rungs to climb before reaching the very top.

The memo starts with some background to the announcement: '. . .wanting to give you continued visibility of our growth platform agenda . . .' it says. Visibility is the latest thing in business. Companies and executives all crave it but, until last week, I didn't know that growth platform agendas were after it too. What is he saying here, I wonder? I think, though couldn't swear to it, that he wants to tell his colleagues how the company plans to make more money.

And so to the meat of the memo. 'We are changing the name of the Human Performance service line to Talent & Organization Performance, effective immediately.'

I'm not sure I've ever seen quite so many waffle words crammed together in one sentence

Before you marvel at the stupidity of the name change, note first that departments can't even be called that: they are instead 'service lines'. As for the name, the old one may have been no great shakes, but to take away the 'human' (which was surely the point) and replace it with 'talent and organisation' is not progress. As I've often remarked before, the word 'talent' is a hideous misnomer as most people aren't terribly talented at all.

Next comes the business rationale for the change. 'With the rise of the multi-polar world, the task of finding and managing talent has become more complex, turbulent and contradictory than ever before.'

This conflicts with two laws, the first of geography – there are only two poles – and the second of business – finding 'talent' has always been hard as there isn't enough to go round. The only excuse for saying it is 'complex, turbulent and contradictory' is to make it sound so complicated that the services of Accenture must be needed to sort it out.

Mr Foster says that what must be done is to teach organisations to 'expand their talent management agenda from a narrow and tactical focus on human resources activities around the employee life cycle, to a broad and strategic focus on highly integrated systems of capabilities fundamental to business strategies and operations'. This is shameful, outrageous bilge. HR should be narrow. It should be specifically focused around the employee life cycle (if that means hiring, training, promoting, firing).

His suggestion is frightening. I'm not sure I've ever seen quite so many waffle words crammed together in one sentence. Broad. Strategic. Focus. Highly. Integrated. System. Capabilities. Fundamental. Strategies. Indeed the only words here that are acceptable are 'to', 'and' and 'on'.

I will spare you further long quotes from this dismal memo, which contains much 'stepping up', 'blue water', 'space' and 'walking the talk'. There is an obsession with capabilities. In four different places Mr Foster talks about 'repositioning' them, 'differentiating' them, 'integrating' them and 'evolving' them. This sounds like quite hard work, especially as I'm not quite sure what capabilities are anyway.

There is only one sentence I like – 'Already we are seeing great progress!' – though it would be better still without the gung-ho exclamation mark.

Alas, the claim turns out to be unsubstantiated. The only progress mentioned is that the head of the newly named service line has written a book called *The Talent Powered Organization* and, to celebrate, Accenture is inviting clients to a party on Second Life – which I suppose cuts down on the bar bill.

How much does all this nonsense matter? Accenture isn't selling pensions to widows; if its rich corporate clients are prepared to buy HR services designed for a multi-polar world, that is their lookout.

However, there is something else about the memo that worries me more. Accenture's website reveals that, unlike Martin Lukes, Mr Foster has a classics degree from Oxford. I had always thought the point of studying classics was that it trained your mind and your pen. What this memo shows is that two decades at Accenture have a more potent effect on befuddling the mind than three years of Aeschylus and Horace ever had on sharpening it.

Source: Lucy Kellaway, *Financial Times*, 27 January 2008.

MANA-GEMS

One of us, Henry, collects typographic errors – 'typos', as they are called. (It's easier than collecting antique cars.) He *writes* his books and articles – literally, badly. So when they get typed, almost anything can happen. And now, with the use of email, and him banging away madly at the keyboard, more carnage appears on the screen. A sampling of all this follows. Be prepared: there is a lot of wisdom in serendipity. (Henry would like to express his deep appreciation to his assistants over the past 16 years, Santa Balanca-Rodrigues and Kate Maguire, for their profound contributions to what follows.)

Leadership curse typos

Brief executive
Chief *existence*
The marketing vice *pediment*

The CEO must be an *infirmed* generalist [informed]
Busimanship [from a Swedish colleague]
Bust [Bush]
Confidence [competence]
He just wants to be sure he can add *volume* [value]
The meeting of the Co-operative Hospital Committee should not be *chained* by the president of the board of directors [chaired]
Reading this, you may consider yourself a leader, or on your way to becoming a leader, or at least working for a leader. You pretty well know what leadership is: Stimulating teamwork. Taking the long view. Engendering trust. Setting *curse* [course]

Marginal typos

Crass-cultural management
Stiff management [staff]
Distracted management [distributed]
Marginal work [managerial]
Managerms
Autistic administration [artistic]
Models of *mingling* [managing]
Direct *suspicion* [supervision]
The *hole* question of management [whole]

Panning typos

Strategic *panning*
Strategic *pleasing*
Strategic *peas*
Stuff planners [staff]
Plain things [plan]
Addressing key *pissues*
Destructive competences [distinctive]
Diversifiction [what a difference an 'a' makes]
Planning can be a means to knit *desperate* activities together [disparate]
The strategies that result from *anxious* thought [conscious]
Students do a course in business *stripping* [strategy]
'I wish to look at the *liturgy* – I mean literature – in strategic management' [courtesy of Pierre Brunet, during his thesis defence]
Rumelt calls the traditional view of strategy formation 'a set of *constricts*' [constructs]
Only those who have the wisdom to see the *pat* are able to imagine the future [past]

We too typos

Toos [tools]
The *statistics* quo [status]
Add a feedback *leap* [loop]
Levels of *obstruction* [abstraction]
Formal confrontation [financial information]
The *anus* is on the specialist to investigate the relevance of his own science [onus]
There is *wonderfully* little synthesis in the world of analysis [woefully]
Consultants tend to come at times of *charge* [change]
We could have just taught about technique and be *undone* with it [done]
Based on the belief that high market share is per se more *profile* [profitable]
A little model of decision making: *defying* the issue, designing courses of action, deciding on the final outcome [defining]
Better description in the hands of the intelligent practitioner is the most powerful prescription tool we have, for that is what enables him or her to change the *word* [world]

SUBJECT: NEW ELEMENT FOR PERIODIC TABLE

The heaviest element known to science is Managerium.

This element has no protons or electrons, but has a nucleus composed of 1 neutron, 2 vice-neutrons, 5 junior vice-neutrons, 25 assistant vice-neutrons, and 125 junior assistant vice-neutrons all going round in circles.

Managerium has a half-life of three years, at which time it does not decay but institutes a series of reviews leading to reorganization. Its molecules are held together by means of the exchange of tiny particles known as morons.

Source: Unknown.

POWERPOINT IS EVIL
BY EDWARD TUFTE

Imagine a widely used and expensive prescription drug that promised to make us beautiful but didn't. Instead the drug had frequent, serious side effects: It induced stupidity, turned everyone into bores, wasted time, and degraded the quality and credibility of communication. These side effects would rightly lead to a worldwide product recall.

Yet slideware – computer programs for presentations – is everywhere: in corporate America, in government bureaucracies, even in our schools. Several hundred million copies of Microsoft PowerPoint are churning out trillions of slides each year. Slideware may help speakers outline their talks, but convenience for the speaker can be punishing to both content and audience. The standard PowerPoint presentation elevates format over content, betraying an attitude of commercialism that turns everything into a sales pitch.

Of course, data-driven meetings are nothing new. Years before today's slideware, presentations at companies such as IBM and in the military used bullet lists shown by overhead projectors. But the format has become ubiquitous under PowerPoint, which was created in 1984 and later acquired by Microsoft. PowerPoint's pushy style seeks to set up a speaker's dominance over the audience. The speaker, after all, is making power points with bullets to followers. Could any metaphor be worse? Voicemail menu systems? Billboards? Television? Stalin?

Particularly disturbing is the adoption of the PowerPoint cognitive style in our schools. Rather than learning to write a report using sentences, children are being taught how to formulate client pitches and infomercials. Elementary school PowerPoint exercises (as seen in teacher guides and in student work posted on the Internet) typically consist of 10 to 20 words and a piece of clip art on each slide in a presentation of three to six slides – a total of perhaps 80 words (15 seconds of silent reading) for a week of work. Students would be better off if the schools simply closed down on those days and everyone went to the Exploratorium or wrote an illustrated essay explaining something.

In a business setting, a PowerPoint slide typically shows 40 words, which is about eight seconds' worth of silent reading material. With so little information per slide, many, many slides are needed. Audiences consequently endure a relentless sequentiality, one damn slide after another. When information is stacked in time, it is difficult to understand context and evaluate relationships. Visual reasoning usually works more effectively when relevant information is shown side by side. Often, the more intense the detail, the greater the clarity and understanding. This is especially so for statistical data, where the fundamental analytical act is to make comparisons.

Presentations largely stand or fall on the quality, relevance, and integrity of the content

Consider an important and intriguing table of survival rates for those with cancer relative to those without cancer for the same time period. Some 196 numbers and 57 words describe survival rates and their standard errors for 24 cancers.

Applying the PowerPoint templates to this nice, straightforward table yields an analytical disaster. The data explodes into six separate chaotic slides, consuming 2.9 times the area of the table. Everything is wrong with these smarmy, incoherent graphs: the encoded legends, the meaningless color, the logo-type branding. They are uncomparative, indifferent to content and evidence, and so data-starved as to be almost pointless. Chartjunk is a clear

Good

Estimates of relative survival rates, by cancer site [19]

	% survival rates and their standard errors							
	5 year		10 year		15 year		20 year	
Prostate	98.8	0.4	95.2	0.9	87.1	1.7	81.1	3.0
Thyroid	96.0	0.8	95.8	1.2	94.0	1.6	95.4	2.1
Testis	94.7	1.1	94.0	1.3	91.1	1.8	88.2	2.3
Melanomas	89.0	0.8	86.7	1.1	83.5	1.5	82.8	1.9
Breast	86.4	0.4	78.3	0.6	71.3	0.7	65.0	1.0
Hodgkin's disease	85.1	1.7	79.8	2.0	73.8	2.4	67.1	2.8
Corpus uteri, uterus	84.3	1.0	83.2	1.3	80.8	1.7	79.2	2.0
Urinary, bladder	82.1	1.0	76.2	1.4	70.3	1.9	67.9	2.4
Cervix, uteri	70.5	1.6	64.1	1.8	62.8	2.1	60.0	2.4
Larynx	68.8	2.1	56.7	2.5	45.8	2.8	37.8	3.1
Rectum	62.6	1.2	55.2	1.4	51.8	1.8	49.2	2.3
Kidney, renal pelvis	61.8	1.3	54.4	1.6	49.8	2.0	47.3	2.6
Colon	61.7	0.8	55.4	1.0	53.9	1.2	52.3	1.6
Non-Hodgkin's	57.8	1.0	46.3	1.2	38.3	1.4	34.3	1.7
Oral cavity, pharynx	56.7	1.3	44.2	1.4	37.5	1.6	33.0	1.8
Ovary	55.0	1.3	49.3	1.6	49.9	1.9	49.6	2.4
Leukemia	42.5	1.2	32.4	1.3	29.7	1.5	26.2	1.7
Brain, nervous system	32.0	1.4	29.2	1.5	27.6	1.6	26.1	1.9
Multiple myeloma	29.5	1.6	12.7	1.5	7.0	1.3	4.8	1.5
Stomach	23.8	1.3	19.4	1.4	19.0	1.7	14.9	1.9
Lung and bronchus	15.0	0.4	10.6	0.4	8.1	0.4	6.5	0.4
Esophagus	14.2	1.4	7.9	1.3	7.7	1.6	5.4	2.0
Liver, bile duct	7.5	1.1	5.8	1.2	6.3	1.5	7.6	2.0
Pancreas	4.0	0.5	3.0	1.5	2.7	0.6	2.7	0.8

A traditional table: rich, informative, clear

Bad

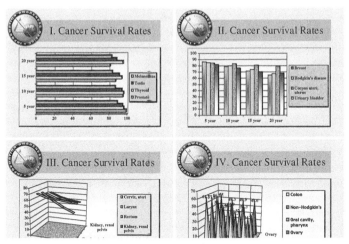

PowerPoint chartjunk: smarmy, chaotic, incoherent

sign of statistical stupidity. Poking a finger into the eye of thought, these data graphics would turn into a nasty travesty if used for a serious purpose, such as helping cancer patients assess their survival chances. To sell a product that messes up data with such systematic intensity, Microsoft abandons any pretense of statistical integrity and reasoning.

Presentations largely stand or fall on the quality, relevance, and integrity of the content. If your numbers are boring, then you've got the wrong numbers.

If your words or images are not on point, making them dance in color won't make them relevant. Audience boredom is usually a content failure, not a decoration failure.

At a minimum, a presentation format should do no harm. Yet the PowerPoint style routinely disrupts, dominates, and trivializes content. Thus PowerPoint presentations too often resemble a school play – very loud, very slow, and very simple.

The practical conclusions are clear. PowerPoint is a competent slide manager and projector. But rather than supplementing a presentation, it has become a substitute for it. Such misuse ignores the most important rule of speaking: Respect your audience.

Reprinted by permission, Edward R. Tufte, *The Cognitive Style of PowerPoint* (Graphics Press, Cheshire, CT, September 2003), as appeared in *Wired* magazine.

PLANNING AS PUBLIC RELATIONS
BY HENRY MINTZBERG

Some organizations use planning as a tool, not because anyone necessarily believes in the value of the process, but because influential outsiders do. Planning becomes a game, called 'public relations'.

Thus 'city governments hire consultants to do "strategic planning" to impress bond rating agencies (Nutt, 1984a: 72) and 'what is frequently called a 'plan' by a university is really an investment brochure;' (Cohen and March, 19). In government, leaders who 'wish to be thought modem … have a document with which to dazzle their visitors.' And why shouldn't they? After all, 'capitalist America insisted upon a plan' in return for its foreign aid to poor countries: 'it did not matter whether the plan worked; what did count was the ability to produce a document which looked like a plan' (Wildavsky, 1973: 140, 151).

In a narrow sense, of course, some of this 'planning' seems to be justified. After all, supermarkets need their capital, the developing nations need their aid, universities need their support. In the poorer nations, national planning 'may be justified on a strictly cash basis: planners may bring in more money from abroad than it costs to support them at home' (Wildavsky, 1973:151).

But in a broader sense, is this kind of planning justified at all? Leaving aside the obvious waste of resources – money that could be saved if everyone stopped playing the game – public relations planning probably distorts priorities. In poor nations, for example, it misallocates skills that are in short supply, and that could be devoted to solving real problems (or doing useful planning). Even in more developed countries, think of how much time and talent has been wasted over the years. Worse, what is intended as public relations can be taken seriously when it should not be.

Add all this together, and public relations planning becomes a means by which almost everyone, no matter how intent on using planning to gain control, ends up losing it. Outsiders get useless pronouncements, and junior managers waste time filling out forms while senior managers get distracted from the more important issues. Only the planners come out on top. And that makes such planning for them fundamentally political.

In the final analysis, in the experiences of western corporations no less than of communist states, planning used for image instead of substance ties everyone in knots and so ends up controlling everybody.

References

Cohen, M. D. and March, J. G., 'Decisions, presidents, and status', in J. G. March and J. P. Olsen (eds), *Ambiguity and Choice in Organizations*, Bergen, Universitetsforlaget, 1976.

Lorrange, P. and Vancil, R. F., *Strategic Planning Systems*, Prentice Hall, 1977.

Nutt, P. C., 'A strategic planning network for non-profit organizations', *Strategic Management Journal*, 1984, 5, 57–75.

Wildavsky, A., 'If planning is everything, maybe it's nothing', *Policy Sciences*, 1973, 4, 127–153.

THE OPPOSITE OF A PROFOUND TRUTH IS ALSO TRUE
BY RICHARD FARSON

Our great achievements in science, law, government, and in every intellectual pursuit are dependent upon our development as rational, logical thinkers.

But this kind of thinking has also limited us. Without quite knowing it, we have become creatures of linear, categorical logic. Things are good or bad, true or false, but not both. We have been taught that a thing cannot be what it is and also it's opposite. Yet it sounds wise when confronted with a conflict to say, 'Well, yes and no.' Or, 'It's both.' We've all heard statements that concede the coexistence of opposites: Less is more. Living is dying. Hating is loving. Although it seems illogical, no two things are as closely related as opposites.

Going in both directions

What practical value can we get out of that notion? At a mundane level, take, for example, the development of frozen food processing. It led to a rash of predictions about the growth of a fast-food market – predictions that certainly turned out to be correct. What was not predicted, however, was the popularity of gourmet cookbooks, with their emphasis on fresh ingredients, organically grown products, wholesome preparation, and a new respect for chefs. Frozen food processing made possible the development of fast food, but along with that development came its opposite.

We have seen the coexistence of opposites in management with the introduction of participative approaches designed to democratize the workplace. These approaches often do increase worker participation. But it is also true that hierarchy and authority remain very much in place, perhaps stronger than ever. That is because the executives who grant the work force some amount of authority never lose any of their own authority. Granting authority is not like handing out a piece of pie, wherein you lose what you give away. It is more like what happens when you give information to someone. Although he or she may now know more, you do not know any less.

Practical deceptions

Another coexistence of opposites: To be healthy, an organization needs full and accurate communication among its members. But also, to be healthy, it needs distortion and deception. If those words sound overly harsh, think of commonly used terms like *diplomacy* and *tact,* which imply less than candid communication.

Just as the profession of medicine or the conduct of a romance requires mystique – that is, encouraging beliefs about oneself that may not be completely accurate but make others feel positively – so, too, do leadership and management. Some, for example, hold that one function of middle management is to massage or filter information, both upward and downward. Such 'distortion' or 'deception' is said to serve two practical purposes.

First, workers are led to believe that their leaders are confident, fair, and capable, reinforcing the necessary myths of leadership. Second, since the top leaders surely would be troubled by knowing everything that goes on in the organization, they are protected from hearing about the petty problems and minor failures of the work force.

In human affairs, some form of deception is the rule, not the exception

In human affairs, some form of deception is the rule, not the exception. In most cases it should not be considered lying, because that term fails to take into account the complexity of human communication and the many ways people must maneuver to keep relationships on an even keel. Appreciating the coexistence of opposites helps us understand that honesty and deception can function together in some paradoxical way.

Contradictory impulses

One executive I know is a classic example of a man who wants to succeed but at the same time seems to want to fail. Everything he does carries both messages. From the very moment he enthusiastically volunteers to head a project, he operates in such a way as to cripple it – refusing to delegate, undermining the work of committees, failing to meet deadlines, and stalling on crucial decisions.

His behavior is not that unusual. Contradictory impulses to both succeed and fail can be found in every project, every work team, even every individual. Every management choice, job offer, or new applicant can appear both appealing and unappealing. Every deal is both good and bad. That is why leadership is essentially the management of dilemmas, why tolerance for ambiguity – coping with contradictions – is essential for leaders, and why appreciating the coexistence of opposites is crucial to the development of a different way of thinking.

Like one

There is yet another spin to this paradox that I have always found intriguing – that opposites not only can coexist, but can even *enhance* one another. Take pleasure and pain, for example. Scratching an itch is both. Not pleasure, then pain, or pain then pleasure, but both at once. Granted, scratching an itch too long can become very painful and no longer pleasurable, but there is a moment when they coexist, when they are one. Like truth and falsity, good and evil.

Source: Richard Farson, *Management of the Absurd*, Simon and Schuster, 1997, pp. 21–24.

SYSTEMATIC BUZZ WORD GENERATOR
BY LEW GLOIN

Functional digital options

We have a wonderful place of jargon that came this way from (it is alleged), the U.S. Public Health Service. There, an official named Philip Broughton, nearing retirement put together a 'sure-fire method for converting frustration into fulfilment (jargon wise)'. He calls the method, the Systematic Buzz Phrase Projector.

It consists of a lexicon of 30 carefully chosen buzzwords, which you, as a jargonaut, may wish to drop into memos, reports or the boss' speeches.

The SBPP is simple to use. Just think of any three-digit number, then select the corresponding buzzword from each list.

List 1	List 2	List 3
0 integrated	**0** management	**0** options
1 total	**1** organizational	**1** flexibility
2 systematized	**2** monitored	**2** capability
3 parallel	**3** reciprocal	**3** nobility
4 functional	**4** digital	**4** programming
5 responsive	**5** logistical	**5** concept
6 optional	**6** transitional	**6** time-phase
7 synchronized	**7** incremental	**7** projection
8 compatible	**8** third-generation	**8** hardware
9 balanced	**9** policy	**9** contingency

For instance, 125 produces total monitored concept. And 440 produces the heading on this column. See how easy it is? You, too, can write authoritative-sounding memos and reports that mean absolutely nothing.

Ron Webster of Brighton writes with a problem: 'Wondered if you could identify the word, the dictionary definition of which is, "product of a mellow world, in which everyone abides by the rules." Read an article years ago, which used the word to describe a person and try as I might, have been unable to recollect the word.'

Okay. Words admits failure. Answer, anyone?

Source: Lew Gloin, 'Words', *Saturday Magazine, The Toronto Star*, 25 February 1989, p. M2.

If everyone is thinking alike, then no-one is thinking.
Benjamin Franklin

CHAPTER 3
MISLEADING MANAGEMENT

Management is the delusion that you can change people. Leadership is deluding other people instead of deluding yourself. [Scott Adams, in Dilbert and the Way of the Weasel]

Leadership: it's all the rage. Amazon has something like 10 000 books on leadership, and hardly more than a handful on followership. Find an organisation with a problem and leadership is inevitably the professed solution. But what if leadership is the problem? Or, at least, what if leadership too is not what we think? Read this chapter, and you might wonder about this too.

So we selected pieces for this chapter that bring leadership down to earth. To open, we turn to Farson again. He challenges the stereotyped image of the leader, conjuring up instead a more realistic picture of leadership distributed among a group.

Next comes an example of this in an interview with John Mackey about how Whole Foods was developed. Not how you might have thought. John Kay reinforces this point with his column in the Financial Times *about how 'A star executive does not make a company'. There are grave dangers in believing that 'supremely talented individuals can single-handedly transform business'.*

Henry Mintzberg follows with some rules for being a 'heroic' (destructive) leader. After this, it's back up the mountain of leadership, about the need for some good sense in literally going up the mountain. We then close this chapter with a plea for more 'communityship' alongside 'just enough leadership'.

THERE ARE NO LEADERS, THERE IS ONLY LEADERSHIP
BY RICHARD FARSON

One of the great enemies of organizational effectiveness is our stereotypical image of a leader. We imagine a commanding figure perhaps standing in front of an audience, talking not listening with an entourage of assistants standing by. Or sitting behind a large clean desk, barking out orders, taking charge – aggressive, no-nonsense, a bulldog.

Such images of leaders get us into trouble not just because they fail to conform to reality, but because they set us up for roles that are ultimately dysfunctional. The macho image of leadership, associated with men like Vince Lombardi, Ross Perot, and Lee Iacocca, makes us forget that the real strength of a leader is the ability to elicit the strength of the group.

Relying on one person to provide all the leadership builds expectations that cannot be met

This paradox is another way of saying that leadership is less the property of a person than the property of a group. Leadership is distributed among members of a group, and they in turn play such vital roles as taskmaster, clown mother figure, and so on. Relying on one person – the manager for example – to provide all the leadership builds expectations that cannot be met. Moreover it robs the group of its powers, leading to overdependence on the manager. In turn, the leader's response to this dependence is sometimes to micromanage, getting into areas of control and responsibility that represent a poor use of time and may far exceed his or her capabilities, actually reducing the productivity of the group.

Defined by the group

People who are leaders in one situation usually are followers in others. For example, they may be managers at work but just interested parents at a PTA meeting, or mere spectators at social gatherings. Leadership is situational, less a personal quality than specific to a situation.

True leaders are defined by the groups they are serving, and they understand the job as being interdependent with the group. We have all seen leaders who successfully move from one organization to another even though they may not be expert in the second organization's business. They are able to do this because they define their task as evoking the knowledge, skills, and creativity of those who are already with the organization. They are secure enough in their own identities to be able to be influenced by new information and to accept the ideas of others in the group. They are especially able to elicit the intelligence and participation of group members who otherwise might not join the discussions.

In a well-functioning group, the behavior of the leader is not all that different from the behavior of other responsible group members. In fact, if it were not for the trappings of titles, private corner offices, desks with overhangs, a seat at the head of the table, and so on, it might be difficult to identify the leader in a group that is working well.

Making life easier

The best leaders are servants of their people. I once conducted a study aimed at trying to understand how people achieve power in a group. We found that those people who were most successful served it. They would go to the blackboard and perform what might be thought as secretarial task for the group. They would call on those who had not spoken; they listened attentively to everyone. They spoke their own views clearly and fully, but mostly they encouraged others to speak theirs. They helped the group to stay focused on the problem. In other words, they tried to serve the group.

Humility comes naturally to the best leaders: They seldom take credit themselves but instead give credit to the group with which they have worked. They characteristically make life easier for their employees. They are constantly arranging situations, engineering jobs, smoothing out the processes, removing the barriers. They think about who needs what. They define their job as finding ways of releasing the creative potential that exists within each individual employee and in each group with which they work . . .

Leaders we don't recognize

We forget sometimes that leadership is a shared role played partly by people who are not titular leaders. Kings have regents whispering in their ears. Presidents have advisers. CEOs have consultants. Managers have assistants who help shape their behavior but who do not take the risks of leadership and who do not get the credit.

Indeed, leaders are themselves often led and managed by their employees, from the bottom up – colleagues whose ideas, assistance, arguments, and sometimes dogged resistance have real influence. Watching an accomplished executive secretary at work can make one wonder sometimes just who is managing whom.

I have found that there are two kinds of good employees. One is the willing assistant prepared to accept whatever tasks are assigned and to accomplish them with dispatch and good will. The other goes further, anticipating what the needs are going to be and then offering solutions, not problems, ideas, not complaints. This anticipatory role is seldom asked for; nevertheless, it is an important leadership role played by those who are not called leaders.

The most powerful force

Most of the actions of leaders don't work, just as most surfers miss more waves than they catch. To complicate matters, there are so many different kinds and styles of leadership, and the actions called for are so complex, that there is no sure model to follow.

Yet leadership is the most powerful force on earth. Arguments can be made for other forces – greed, territoriality, guilt, fear, hate, love, spirituality – but without leadership to mobilize them, they are relatively weak. Leadership, therefore, deserves a great deal more attention than it has been given, especially if we want to make certain that it is exercised in ways that help our organizations thrive and our civilization progress.

Source: Richard Farson, *Management of the Absurd*, Simon and Schuster, 1997, pp. 144–147.

CONVERSATIONS FROM THE CORNER OFFICE
JOHN MACKEY TALKS WITH KAI RYSSDAL

KAI RYSSDAL: John Mackey welcome to the program.

JOHN MACKEY: Thanks. Good to be here.

RYSSDAL: So I had a couple of hours to kill before you and I sat down; so I went downstairs to look for lunch and two things happened. One was I couldn't figure out what to eat because this place has so much in it; but the other one was I kind of got lost because it's so big. Is this what you had in mind 25 years ago?

MACKEY: No. Twenty-five years ago? No . . . There's a misconception somehow or another that there was some, like, master plan and I've been, like, fulfilling the master plan that we made up 25 years ago, but . . . it's a discovery process. We've been making it up as we go along.

I can't tell you exactly how the company will be in five years. I think most CEOs who tell you where their company is going to be in five years either are making a big mistake or they're lying.

RYSSDAL: But surely you have some strategic plan for this company . . . it's not just bigger and more, right?

MACKEY: Well, I mean, it's more like imagine for a second . . . there's not like a map, that we're following this map, it's more like we're writing the map as we go along. So we keep learning, so we keep changing the plan. Well, I'll give you a great example.

In June we're going to open our biggest store we've ever opened in London. It's a great location in London. Now, if that store does extremely well, and we think it will, and if it does really well, say as good as our New York stores do, then we're going to do a lot more stores in the UK, and we'll probably try to do one in another capital in Europe, say in some place like Amsterdam, or Hamburg or Paris or Milan or something like that.

If the store bombs then we'll certainly rethink how aggressively we're going to go into Europe. So that is a big experiment and the results of the experiment will sort of tell us where we'll be going. Our first store in New York was very successful. If it hadn't been successful we wouldn't have all those other stores in New York and we wouldn't have several other stores in development there. So the plan continues to evolve. In other words, we keep making it up as we gain more information.

RYSSDAL: What was the short-term plan when you guys sat down and said let's start a company called Whole Foods Market?

MACKEY: Well, we didn't have a plan. My girlfriend and I started it . . . because we thought it would be fun. It was an adventure. Imagine a couple of young people that are taking backpacks and going to Europe and they know they've got three months over there but they don't necessarily have a complete itinerary worked out, exactly where they're going to go because they don't know who they're going to meet and they don't know what kind of adventures they're going to have . . . [T]he plan will unfold as they go along.

That's kind of how Whole Foods has been.

RYSSDAL: Why groceries and food? Why not shoes or clothing or anything else?

MACKEY: Well, that's a fair question. I got interested in food when I was in my early 20s. I moved into this vegetarian co-op to live . . . I wasn't a vegetarian, but I figured the co-op would have a lot of interesting women living there.
[Laughter]
And . . .

RYSSDAL: And?

MACKEY: And they did . . . I met my girlfriend that I started the company with at the co-op, so I learned how to cook and I became the food buyer, I got very interested in food, I sort of had a food awakening about what's happened to our food over the years, [how] . . . our food supply has become more industrialized; I learned about organics, I learned how to cook. And so I got very interested in food.

And so . . . I went to work for a small natural foods store, first time I'd ever worked in one, and first time I'd ever worked in a retail store, and I really liked it. I pitched the idea to my girlfriend . . . hey, why don't we go do our own small store and she loved it and we went out and hustled everybody we knew and raised $45,000 and opened the first store.

RYSSDAL: And had some real problems with that first store? . . .

MACKEY: We didn't know what we were doing . . . we lost $23,000, so half the money in the first year we lost. But . . . I'm a quick learner, so we made a small profit in the year two, and . . . the first thing I realized was the store was too small and we needed to get to a larger location if we were really going to be successful and compete.

RYSSDAL: It's funny, because that's not one of those intuitive things. You don't necessarily think if you're running a business, man, we've got to be bigger to succeed.

MACKEY: That's exactly what the investors told me.
[Laughter]
They said look, I'm glad we're profitable now, John, or we're glad you're profitable now . . . why don't we stay here for a few years and get some of our investment back and I said well, because I don't think we'll be competitive here over the long-term. They still didn't want to do it and basically they said look, we don't want to put any more money in it this time, but if you could find other investors, we'll consider it. And their basic strategy was that they didn't think anybody would be stupid enough to invest in this business . . . [B]ut I was very persuasive.
I think entrepreneurs really believe in their dreams and they're able to sell them and persuade other people to go along with the dream.

RYSSDAL: How did becoming an entrepreneur change you?

MACKEY: How didn't it change me? I mean, I'm completely a different person now than I was when I was 24-years-old . . . [W]hatever choices you make in life affect you. I mean they change you. I've learned a lot more about people; I've learned a lot more about myself. I've certainly learned a lot about business. I've grown tremendously. I think. As a human being. I'm wiser and kinder and more loving and a better leader.
I'm a little bit more mature now than I was when I was 24 although my wife might argue with me on that.

RYSSDAL: It might be worth a mention here that you've got no business background per se. There's no MBA there, there's no, you know, none of that.

MACKEY: I have the perfect background, I've studied philosophy.
[Laughter]

RYSSDAL: Excellent.

MACKEY: And so I didn't have any biases . . . I didn't know how it was 'supposed' to be done. I didn't have any preconceptions about how business had to be. So that . . . meant I made mistakes, I reinvented . . . we reinvented the wheel a few times but I didn't know what I couldn't do.

And so I was free . . . we were free to be creative and inventive and try new ways of doing things and . . . Whole Foods is innovative in lots of different ways, it's a different kind of organization than most other corporations.

RYSSDAL: In fact, I think I read some place while doing some research for this that year-over-year thinking innovation is the key now to Whole Foods' future, to keep it growing the way it has been.

MACKEY: Yeah, it is.

RYSSDAL: What's left in this space to innovate besides more organic and more naturalness?

MACKEY: Well, I mean, I'm going to give you an evasive answer on that. It's sort of like when you asked the question about the plan . . . do I know the plan for the long-term and I don't know what the innovations are . . . if I already knew what they were we'd already done it, right? Creativity is something that comes from within us and it's somewhat of a mysterious process, I mean, there's certainly a lot of studies been done on it, but you put disparate pieces of information together and new combinations come up and voilà, you have creativity.

The main thing is that Whole Foods has this experimental, innovative attitude so we're constantly trying new things. Every store in a way is an experiment and the reason that's important is that unlike most other retailers, let's take . . . Starbucks or McDonald's, for example, they come up with a prototype store and then they just replicate it over and over and over again so it's not that they don't ever make any changes, they might evolve their prototype, but then again they're still kind of stamping out like the cookies, a very similar type store.

We're more like custom home builders, . . . every store is unique, every store is an experiment, every store is creating new innovations, so we're not just doing the same thing over and over and over again.

Source: Excerpted from interview transcript: American Public Media's *Market Place*, 26 February 2007, Whole Foods CEO John Mackey talks with Kai Ryssdal.

A STAR EXECUTIVE DOES NOT MAKE A COMPANY
BY JOHN KAY

The share price of Hewlett-Packard jumped when Carly Fiorina was appointed chief executive in 1999 and it jumped again when she was fired last week. In the meantime, it fell by more than half.

Ms Fiorina was headhunted by Hewlett-Packard from Lucent, then flying high. HP, once the most revered name in Silicon Valley, was looking for an exceptional person to restore the company's fortunes. Ms Fiorina, who had reportedly stuffed crumpled socks in her pants to show the sales people that she had balls, apparently met this requirement.

Beauty contests for executive talent are common today. The competitive hunt for the best people in other companies supposes that general management skills are more important than specific organisational knowledge and that supremely talented individuals can single-handedly transform businesses with their vision and charisma. Rakesh Khurana's *Searching for a Corporate Saviour* and Henry Mintzberg's *Managers not MBAs* cruelly dissect these fallacies.

Ms Fiorina did the things expected of transformational leaders. She embarked on a public relations offensive. Within the company, 'coffee with Carly' took over from 'the HP way'. On public appearances, the immaculately tousled hair of America's leading female executive quickly made her the most readily recognised business figure in the country.

She demanded rounds of cost reduction from subordinates. Sometimes such economies lead to greater efficiency, sometimes they undermine the long-term prospects of the business. In the absence of intimate knowledge of the organisation in question, it is hard to tell. No matter: in either case the process enhances earnings per share in the short run.

But the real test of the corporate saviour is whether she can land the big deal. Ms Fiorina first made a pitch for the consulting business of PwC, only to learn that many of the opinionated folk in that business were unenthusiastic about a merger with a manufacturing company under her leadership. But she completed the acquisition of the ailing Compaq. The results were disappointing and last week Ms Fiorina paid the price.

The lesson from Hewlett-Packard is not simply that Ms Fiorina was not up to the job. It is that the role in which she so willingly cast herself is not one in which anyone is likely to succeed.

Great businesses depend on the talents of thousands of people, not just one

It is not always a mistake to hire an outsider for the top job. This move can be effective when the culture of an organisation has become so dysfunctional that it is almost necessary to start again. But the outsider who brings his or her own blueprint will almost invariably fail: the better approach to this task is to find and release the frustrated energy already present in the business. As the American pro-consuls in Iraq can testify, such reconstruction is no easy task. There is also a business role for larger-than-life personalities – such as Bill Hewlett or Dave Packard. Such figures make their principal contribution in the early stages of corporate development, when the positioning, identity and values of the business need to be established.

But there is a world of difference between the attributes appropriate to the founding entrepreneur and the political skills demanded of the effective manager of a larger organisation. Henry Ford defined the products and technology of the car industry but Alfred Sloan at General Motors defined the structures needed to run it, something of which Ford himself was quite incapable. It has been fashionable – and lucrative – for consultants, gurus and especially chief executives to blur this distinction between the entrepreneur and the professional manager. But the results of that elision have generally – as at HP – been unsuccessful and frequently – as at WorldCom or Vivendi – disastrous.

Great businesses depend on the talents of thousands of people, not just one. Their management requires a multiplicity of incompatible talents: both vision and attention to detail, both emotional intelligence and analytic capability, both self-confidence and self-criticism. The most effective managers possess an idiosyncratic balance of attributes appropriate for the situations they face, and the range of abilities successful companies require must be sought across a team rather than in a single personality. Rows of suits are less photogenic than Carly Fiorina but they are what really makes modern business work.

Source: John Kay, *Financial Times*, 15 February 2005.

RULES FOR BEING A HEROIC LEADER
BY HENRY MINTZBERG

- Look out, not in. Ignore the existing business as much as possible, since anything established takes time to fix. Leave that to whoever was not downsized.

- Be dramatic. Do the deal and promise the world, to catch the attention of the investment community. In particular, merge like mad: go after other established businesses – the devils you don't know.

- Focus on the present. The past is gone, dead, and the future is distant. Do that dramatic deal *now*.

- Inside the company, favor outsiders over insiders; anyone who knows the business is suspect. Bring in a whole new 'top team'. Rely especially on consultants – they appreciate heroic leaders.

- To drive the insiders, use the numbers. That way you do not have to manage performance so much as deem it.

- Promote the changing of everything all the time. In particular, reorganize constantly; it keeps everyone on their toes (instead of planted on their feet). Refuse to change this behavior no matter what the consequences.

- Be a risk taker. Your golden parachute will protect you.

- Above all, get that stock price up. Then cash in and run. Heroes are in great demand.

Source: Henry Mintzberg, 'Heroic leader', in *Managers not MBAs: A hard look at the soft practice of managing and management development*, FT/Prentice Hall, 2004, pp. 110–111.

A DESCENT IN THE DARK
BY R.R. RENO

. . . Climbers use a term from romantic life to describe the difference: commitment. At the local crag, if you get tired in the early afternoon or if storm clouds threaten, then you can call it quits and head home for an early beer. On a big climb it's not so simple. The commitment is not just a matter of size and difficulty. In the mountains, weather, glaciers, and rock fall create a dangerous environment. Climbers need to move quickly, not only in order to complete a long climb in a reasonable period of time but more importantly to minimize exposure to danger. Speed equals safety, and serious mountain climbers need to be decisive, bold, and confident. There's no time for extra safety precautions.

The element of commitment is what makes for adventure. You set for yourself an objective that cannot easily be attained – and one in which failure will bring a great deal of suffering – and then you kick away the obvious supports and block the ready avenues of escape. Rather than assembling a crew on a larger, safer boat, the sailor sets out solo across the Atlantic Ocean. Rather than the sunny, gentle ridge to the summit, the mountaineer chooses the dark, dangerous north face.

These choices are mysterious, but I don't think they are unfamiliar. The term *adventurer* was first used to describe the soldier of fortune, the man who entertains the dangers of battle not in order to defend his homeland or fulfill his duty, not even for the sake of conquest and booty, but to live as one who risks death. He takes his chances. He romances *Fortuna*, confident that his skill with the sword will carry him through.

> ### Anybody who has drunk enough beer can strap on a bungee harness and throw himself off a bridge

To a great extent, this basic meaning of adventure has remained constant, even as the range of activities we think of as adventuresome has expanded far beyond the exploits of d'Artagnan and his comrades. That is why mountain climbing or solo sailing or extreme skiing is not at all like the thrill-seeking of bungee jumping, or simply a matter of collecting summits. Anybody who has drunk enough beer can strap on a bungee harness and throw himself off a bridge; once you jump, the rest is just an exercise in screaming and letting the carnival-like mechanism do its work. As for summits, you can drive up Pike's Peak or take a helicopter to the top of the Grand Teton. Serious climbing is about getting to the top by a route that tests your competence with difficulty – and your will with danger.

A true adventurer is not foolhardy. He must realistically assess his capabilities and choose reasonable objectives. The sailor looks at himself and weighs his skills, and only then decides that he can cross the Atlantic in a smaller boat. The climber takes an inventory of his experience and judges himself capable of more remote peaks by more difficult routes. But as soon as the next step is taken, the margin of safety decreases. Bad weather, bad decisions, bad luck – all these factors crowd in more and more closely against competence and determination. That's why the best adventures involve a strange combination of emotions: a strong expectation of success in concert with all sorts of doubts and worries about the consequences of failure . . .

Source: R.R. Reno, 'A descent in the dark', CommentaryMagazine.com, November 2008.

LEADERSHIP AND COMMUNITYSHIP
BY HENRY MINTZBERG

We have this obsession with 'leadership'. It's maybe intended to empower people, but its effect is to disempower them. By focusing on the individual, even in the context of others, leadership can undermine a service of community. This is part of the syndrome of individuality that is sweeping the world and undermining organizations in particular and societies in general.

Just enough leadership

Of course leadership matters. And of course leadership can make a difference. But how often does this get magnified into a tautology: show the press a successful organization and it will show you a great leader. So much easier than trying to find out what has really been going on. 'In four years Gerstner has added more than $40 billion to IBM's share value', proclaimed *Fortune* magazine in 1997 (April 14). All by himself!

Where leadership does matter, as it probably did in Gerstner's case, what kind of leadership is that? Is it the heroic leadership so commonly portrayed in the press – the great one who rides in on the great white horse to save the day, even if he or she only arrived yesterday, with barely any knowledge of the organization, its history, its culture? This has more often proved to be a formula for disaster. According to one report ("Waking Up IBM" by Gary Hamel, Harvard Business Review, 7–8, 2000), IBM got into E-business because a programmer with an idea convinced a staff manager, who had more insight than budget, stitched together a team that drove the change. And what role did Gerstner play? When he eventually heard about the initiative, he encouraged it. That's all. Instead of setting direction, he supported the direction setting of others. He provided less leadership. But appropriate leadership. Just enough leadership! What could be simpler, more natural, than that?

For starters, let's recognize that separating leadership from management is part of the problem. Does anyone want to work for a manager who lacks the qualities of leadership? That can be pretty discouraging. Well, how about a leader who doesn't practice management? That can be pretty alienating: he or she is unlikely to know what is going on. (These days, we distinguish leaders from managers. Half a century ago, Peter Drucker distinguished managers from administrators – and had exactly the same idea in mind! We keep upping the ante – soon we will be separating gods for heroes.)

We hear a great deal about micro managing these days – managers who meddle in the work of their reports. Sure it can be a problem. But far more serious now is macro managing – managers who sit on "top," pronouncing their grand visions, great strategies, and stifle performance standards, while everyone else is supposed to scurry around "implementing". I call this management by deeming.

We have too much disconnected leadership in this world – the hyped-up, individually focused, context-free leadership so popular in the press and the classroom. Courses and MBA programs that claim to create leaders promote hubris instead. No leader has ever been created in a classroom. Leadership grows in context, where it gains its most important characteristic: legitimacy. Enough of all these young, barely experienced people running around calling themselves "leaders", worse still "young leaders" (who can really discern that?), just because some course or institution spilled the holy water of "leadership" on people they hardly knew.

Imposed vs. Earned Leadership

Mostly these days, we got illegitimate leadership, selected by outsiders and imposed on an organization or one of its units. A board of mostly outside directors, or a senior management gets charmed by a candidate whose internal practice of management they have never experienced. How remarkable that those people who know the candidates best, having been led, or at least managed, by them, are so rarely consulted on these choices. The current American ambassador to the United Nations was described in the congressional hearings on selection: as "a kiss-up and kick-down" sort of guy. The world is now loaded with such "leaders."

True leadership is earned, internally, if you like – in the unit, or the organization, or even the nation that not only accepts the guidance of some person, but sought it out in the first place, and has subsequently sustained it enthusiastically. How many of today's companies and countries can claim to be headed by people with that kind of legitimacy? How many current heads of state have been "drafted" by overwhelmingly popular will, as, say, Nelson Mandela in South Africa?

"Community-ship"

But even this overstates the case for leadership. People, of course, seek leaders, But often they fool themselves, by mixing up leaders with leadership. There is, in other words, need for more of what is called "distributed leadership," meaning that the role is fluid, shared by various people in a group according to their capabilities as conditions change. Is that not how the Linux Operating System and Wikipedia work?

But calling this leadership really slights it, because its effectiveness lies not in any individuals so much as in the collective social process – essentially in community. Every time we use the word leadership, therefore, we have to bear in mind that it isolates the individual while considering everyone else a follower. Is this the kind of world we want: overwhelmingly of followers? Will that make our institutions and/or societies better places?

Our obsession with leadership, of any kind, causes us to build organizations that are utterly dependent on individual initiative. We don't allow them to function as communities. So when they fail, we blame the leader, and seek a better one. Like drug addicts, each time we just need a bigger bit.

Just consider that ubiquitous organization char, with its silly boxes of "top", "middle", and "bottom" managers. This is no more than a distorted metaphor. What does it tell us, beside who has authority over what. The painting may not be the pipe, but far too many people, this chart is the organization.) Isn't it time we began to think of our organizations as communities of cooperation. And in so doing, put leadership in its place: not gone, but alongside other important social processes.

Isn't it time we began to think of our organizations as communities of cooperation, and in so doing put leadership in its place: not gone, but alongside other important social processes

What should be gone is this magic bullet of the individual as the solution to the world's problems. We are the solution to the world's problems, you and me, all of us, working in concert. In fact, this obsession with leadership is the cause of many of the world's problems.

And with this, get rid of the cult of leadership, striking at least one blow at our increasing obsession with individuality. Not to create a new cult around distributed leadership, but to recognize that the very use of the word leadership tilts thinking toward the individual and away from the community. We don't only need better leadership, we also need less leadership.

How about if we challenge every single speech, program, article, and book that uses the word "leadership" and does not give equal attention to "community-ship" in one form or another? This could have profound implications, not only for the effectiveness of our organizations, but also for the democracy of our societies.

Source: Parts of this were published as 'Enough leadership' in the *Harvard Business Review* (November 2004) and the *Financial Times* (November 2004). Reprinted by permission of *Harvard Business Review*, © by the Harvard Business School Publishing Corporation; all rights reserved.

The hero doth like the ape, that, the higher he climbs, the more he shows his arse. Sir Francis Bacon

CHAPTER 4
MYTHS OF MANAGING

Year after year the worriers and fretters would come to me with awful predictions of the outbreak of war. I denied it each time. I was only wrong twice [Researcher in British Foreign Office from 1903 to 1950.]

Now it's straight into the myths of managing. Management has had a long-standing love affair with formal rationality. 'Crunch the numbers', introduce the right systems, do your action plan (an oxymoron), and the Holy Grail of managing will be yours. How to explain this? Perhaps it reflects our obsession with control – having to bring under control at first things physical, then things social, and finally each other. Or maybe it's all about our desperate search for comfort and security in the face of uncertainty.

We had great fun choosing these pieces. Our first myth takes a light-hearted look at the fad of the decade – outsourcing. Coming to your organisation soon could be the out-sourcing of your CEO. Why not? This person may be the only one left. Then Danny Miller and Jon Hartwick consider why management fads are so popular, concluding that 'If it looks too simple to work, it probably is.' Next Henry Mintzberg muses on a number of management myths, including 'the soft underbelly of hard data', concluding with a shot at the very places that perpetrate these myths.

Scholars have long been fascinated by the biases and distortions we exhibit, especially in processing information. Spyros Makridakis, a leading authority on forecasting, demonstrates rather depressingly how these plague so many of our decisions.

Be that as it may, the architects of these decisions – those swash-buckling CEOs – continue to pile in the money. Why? Because they are bold, risk-taking gamblers, many of them tell us. Once again: think again. 'Some gamblers' concludes by calling the bluff of these high-rolling CEOs. But fear not. While these CEOs seem always to win, surrounded as they are by all that money, maybe they are the real losers.

OUTSOURCING THE OUTSOURCERS

Montreal, March 28, 2005. Air Maple Leaf today announced that the Office of the President, CEO and the Chairman will be outsourced as of April 30, for the remainder of this fiscal year and beyond.

'At the end of the day, the cost savings will be quite significant,' says an Air Maple Leaf spokesperson. 'We simply can no longer afford this inefficiency and remain competitive on the world stage,' he said.

Rahdpoor Nahassbaalapan, 23, of Indus Teleservices, Mumbai, India, will be assuming the Office of President, Chairman, and CEO as of May 1. He will receive a salary of $360 Canadian a month with proportionate benefits. Mr. Nahassbaalapan will maintain his office in India and will be working primarily at night, due to the time difference between Canada and India.

'I am excited to serve in this position,' Mr. Nahassbaalapan stated in an exclusive interview. 'I always knew that my career at the Air Maple Leaf call center would lead to great things.'

An Air Maple Leaf spokesperson noted that Mr. Nahassbaalapan has extensive experience in public speaking and has been given the CEO's Script Tree to enable him to answer any question without having to understand the issue.

The Air Maple Leaf board continues to explore other outsourcing possibilities, including Air Maple Leaf's more than 100 vice presidents.

Source: Adapted from an email that circulated in Montreal in the spring of 2005, apparently inspired by similar stories about the US presidency. Its authenticity, let alone source, could not be confirmed.

SPOTTING MANAGEMENT FADS
BY DANNY MILLER AND JON HARTWICK

What makes them so popular is what undermines them in the end.

TQM. MBO. Japanese management. Like fashion trends, management fads erupt on the scene, enjoy a period of prominence, and then are supplanted. What makes business fads so attractive? And how can managers tell a fad from a tool that might endure?

To find out, we studied many of the more popular business fads of the last 40 years, looking for ideas that followed the characteristic trajectory from sudden prominence to obscurity. In reviewing 1,700 academic, professional, business, and trade publications over a 17-year period, we observed the rise and fall of many business fads.

Though the term 'fad' may seem dismissive, it's not: Fads like TQM can profoundly change companies, for better or for worse. And they can introduce useful ideas that companies incorporate into practice, even as the fad itself fades from the scene. But fads often fail to deliver on their promises, a factor that contributes to their short life cycles and rapid decline. In the course of our work, we uncovered eight qualities that most business fads share. Let's look at these qualities as they apply to three fads: total quality management, Japanese management, and management by objective.

Fads are . . .

Simple. Fad concepts are easy to understand and communicate and tend to be framed with labels, buzzwords, lists, and acronyms. Usually, a few key points convey a fundamental message. TQM, for example, rests on five essential pillars. But because fads are by their very nature suited for a simple world, they have limited utility in the real one.

fads often fail to deliver on their promises, a factor that contributes to their short life cycles and rapid decline

Prescriptive. Fads tell managers what to do. MBO, Theory Z, TQM – all indicate specific actions managers must take to solve problems or improve their companies. Though a fad's fundamental ideas might be sound, the need to be simple but prescriptive makes their action points easy to misinterpret or inappropriately apply. What a mistake it would be to blithely adapt Japanese management's lifelong employment and seniority-based promotions to highly specialized technology positions.

Falsely Encouraging. Fads promise outcomes such as greater effectiveness, more motivated and productive workers, and deeply satisfied customers. But, in fact, all kinds of fads are better at raising hopes than delivering results, and they generally fail to specify clear-cut criteria for evaluating whether or not an implementation succeeded.

One-Size-Fits-All. Fads claim universal relevance, proposing practices that adherents say will apply to almost any industry, organization, or culture – from General Motors to government bureaucracies to mom-and-pop groceries. But few management approaches are universally applicable, and attempts to implement a mismatched approach can do more harm than good. Japanese management practices may transplant poorly to other cultures; TQM may be inappropriate for many producers of basic goods.

few management approaches are universally applicable, and attempts to implement a mismatched approach can do more harm than good

Easy to Cut-and-Paste. Because fad management ideas must be simple and easy to apply, they're amenable to partial implementation. For instance, you can get quality circles going simply by having a prescribed number of people attend regular meetings. Partial implementation means that certain fad features can be grafted onto standard operating procedures and localized within a few committees or departments. Outside these pockets, it's business as usual – which means that fads rarely challenge the status quo in a way that would require significant redistribution of power or resources.

In Tune with the Zeitgeist. Fads resonate with the pressing business problems of the day. MBO became popular with the advent of diversified businesses that demanded coordination and control from generalist managers. Japanese management caught on when the United States began losing market share to Japanese and European companies, often because U.S. products lacked quality. Because fads focus on the concerns of the moment, they tend to apply to a few specific issues rather than addressing the fundamental weakness or soundness of overall business practices.

Novel, not Radical. Fads grab attention by their apparent novelty. But their freshness is often superficial, and, as such, fads don't unduly challenge basic managerial values. Many simply repackage or extend ideas or approaches that managers have long embraced. MBO took much from the planning literature; the one-minute manager idea borrowed from MBO; Theory Z tapped Theory X.

Legitimized by Gurus and Disciples. Many fads gain credibility by the status and prestige of their proponents or followers, rather than through empirical evidence. And stories of corporate heroes and organizational successes suggest prestigious adherents. For example, consultant W. Edwards Deming is inextricably linked with TQM as the architect of the 14 Points for Management.

The very characteristics that make fads popular also contribute to their decline. Their simplicity, presumed generality, and promise of results that often don't materialize virtually guarantee that they'll fall short of managers' expectations – and soon be abandoned.

Classic qualities

If these are the earmarks of fads, what makes a management classic? Consider diversification, decentralization, outsourcing, and supply chain management. Unlike most fads, these likely classics demand real organizational changes at significant cost and have lasting effects. Classics typically arise not from the writings of academics or consultants but emerge out of practitioner responses to economic, social, and competitive challenges. They are complex, multifaceted, and applied in different ways to different businesses. The classics don't come with simple primers on how to make the changes they propose nor do they have simple rules everyone must follow or any guaranteed outcomes.

There is no perfect test to distinguish fads from classics; indeed, their features can overlap. Fads can sometimes trigger major organizational change, even if they're short-lived. And classics, of course, can have gurus – think of Peter Drucker's association with decentralization. But, if a management approach shares most of the fad features described here, beware. If it looks too simple to work, it probably is.

So when managers evaluate a business approach or technique, they should ask these questions: Does the approach have a track record for performance and measurable outcomes in similar companies facing similar challenges? Does it address problems or opportunities that are high priorities for our company? Are the changes it would require within our company's capabilities and resources? Yes answers to these questions suggest an approach likely to pay off and endure.

Source: Reprinted by permission of *Harvard Business Review*. From 'Spotting Management Fads' by Danny Miller and Jon Hartwick, 1 October 2002. Copyright © 2002 by the Harvard Business School Publishing Corporation; all rights reserved.

He flung himself from the room, flung himself upon his horse, and rode madly off in all directions. Stephen Leacock

MUSINGS ON MANAGEMENT
BY HENRY MINTZBERG

Management is a curious phenomenon. It is generously paid, enormously influential, and significantly devoid of common sense. At least, the hype about management lacks common sense, as does too much of the practice . . .

These concerns had been building in my mind for years when a particular event caused them to gel. I had been asked to give a speech at the World Economic Forum in Davos, Switzerland, in 1995; so I visited managing director Maria Cattaui in her office near Geneva to discuss possible topics. I first proposed a presentation on government and suggested she allot me the better part of an hour to cover the topic properly. 'I would really prefer you do something on management,' she replied. 'And besides, many chief executives tend to have an attention span of about 15 minutes.'

I went home, thought about this, and decided to respond in kind . . . I listed ten points on one sheet of paper under the label 'Musings on Management' and faxed it to Maria Cattaui. Fortunately, she was open-minded – indeed, enthusiastic. So that was what I presented at Davos: ten points, by then reduced at her request to ten minutes, one musing on management per minute.

The *Harvard Business Review* being even more open-minded, I can now develop my musings at somewhat greater length, except the last one . . .

1. **Organizations don't have tops and bottoms**. These are just misguided metaphors. What organizations really have are the *outer* people, connected to the world, and the *inner* ones, disconnected from it, as well as many so-called *middle* managers, who are desperately trying to connect the inner and outer people to each other.

The sooner we stop talking about top management (nobody dares to say *bottom* management), the better off we shall be. After all, organizations are spread out geographically, so that even if the chief executive sits 100 stories up in New York, he or she is not nearly as high as a lowly clerk on the ground floor in Denver.

The only thing a chief executive sits atop is an organization chart. And all that silly document does is demonstrate how mesmerized we are with the abstraction called management. The next time you look at one of these charts, cover the name of the organization and try to figure out what it actually does for a living. This most prominent of all corporate artifacts never gets down to real products and real services, let alone the people who deal with them every day. It's as if the organization exists for the management.

Try this metaphor. Picture the organization as a circle. In the middle is the *central* management. And around the outer edges are those people who develop, produce, and deliver the products and services – the people with the knowledge of the daily operations. The latter see with complete clarity because they are closest to the action. But they do so only narrowly, for all they can see are their own little segments. The managers at the center see widely – all around the circle – but they don't see clearly because they are distant from the operations. The trick, therefore, is to connect the two groups. And for that, most organizations need informed managers in between, people who can see the outer edge and then swing around and talk about it to those at the center. You know – the people we used to call middle managers, the ones who are mostly gone.

2. **It is time to delayer the delayerers**. As organizations remove layers from their operations, they add them to the so-called top of their hierarchies – new levels that do nothing but exercise financial control and so drive everyone else crazy.

I used to write books for an independent publishing company called Prentice-Hall. It was big – very big – but well organized and absolutely dedicated to its craft. Then it was bought by Simon & Schuster, which was bought by Paramount. Good old Prentice-Hall became a 'Paramount Communications Company'. It was at about this time that one of my editors quoted her new boss as saying, 'We're in the business of filling the O.I. [operating income] bucket.' Strange, because my editor and I both had thought the company was in the business of publishing books and enlightening readers . . . Now Prentice-Hall has become a 'Viacom Company'. After all this, will publishing books remain as important as satisfying bosses? . . .

Listen to what *Fortune* wrote a few years ago: 'What's truly amazing about P&G's historic restructuring is that it is a response to the consumer market, not the stock market' (November 6, 1989). What's truly amazing about this statement is the use of the phrase 'truly amazing'.

Nowhere does the harshness of such attitudes appear more starkly than in the delayering of all those middle managers. Delayering can be defined as the process by which people who barely know what's going on get rid of those who do . . . Isn't it time that we began to delayer the delayerers?

3. **Lean is mean and doesn't even improve long-term profits.** There is nothing wonderful about firing people. True, stock market analysts seem to love companies that fire frontline workers and middle managers (while increasing the salaries of senior executives). Implicitly, employees are blamed for having been hired in the first place and are sentenced to suffer the consequences while the corporations cash in . . .

I did some work recently for a large U.S. insurance company, with no market analysts to worry about because it is a mutual. I was told a story about a woman there who was working energetically to convert a paper database to an electronic one. Someone said to her, 'Don't you know you are working yourself out of a job?' 'Sure,' she retorted. 'But I know they'll find something else for me. If I didn't, I'd sabotage the process.' . . . How much sabotage is going on? . . .

Great strategists are either creative or generous. We have too few of either type

4. **The trouble with most strategies are chief executives who believe themselves to be strategists.** Great strategists are either creative or generous. We have too few of either type. We call the creative ones visionaries – they see a world that others have been blind to. These are often difficult people, but they break new ground in their own ways. The generous ones, in contrast, bring strategy out in other people. They build organizations that foster thoughtful inquiry and creative action. (You can recognize these people by the huge salaries they don't pay themselves.) . . . The creative strategists reach out from the center of that circular organization to touch the edges, while the generous ones strengthen the whole circle by turning strategic thinking into a collective learning process.

Most so-called strategists, however, just sit on top and pretend to strategize. They formulate ever so clever strategies for everyone else to implement. They issue glossy strategic plans that look wonderful and take their organizations nowhere with great fanfare. Strategy becomes a game of chess in which the pieces – great blocks of businesses and companies – get moved around with a ferocity that dazzles the market analysts. All the pieces look like they fit neatly together – at least on the board. It's all very impressive, except that the pieces themselves, ignored as every eye focuses on the great moves, disintegrate. Imagine if we took all this energy spent on shuffling and used it instead to improve *real* businesses. I don't mean 'financial services' or 'communications', I mean banking or book publishing . . .

5. Decentralization centralizes, empowerment disempowers, and measurement doesn't measure up. The buzzwords are the problem, not the solution. The hot techniques dazzle us. Then they fizzle. *Total quality management* takes over and no one even remembers *quality of work life* – same word, similar idea, no less the craze, not very long ago . . .

The TQM concept has now magically metamorphosed into empowerment. What empowerment really means is stopping the disempowering of people. But that just brings us back to hierarchy, because hierarchy is precisely what empowerment reinforces. People don't get power because it is logically and intrinsically built into their jobs; they get it as a gift from the gods who sit atop those charts. Noblesse oblige. If you doubt this, then contrast empowerment with a situation in which the workers really do have control. Imagine a hospital director empowering the doctors . . . Better still, consider a truly advanced social system: the beehive. Queen bees don't empower worker bees. The worker bees are adults, so to speak, who know exactly what they have to do. Indeed, the queen bee has no role in the genuinely strategic decisions of the hive, such as the one to move to a new location. The bees decide collectively, responding to the informative dances of the scouts and then swarming off to the place they like best. The queen simply follows. How many of our organizations have attained that level of sophistication? What the queen bee does is exude a chemical substance that holds the system together. She is responsible for what has been called the 'spirit of the hive'. What a wonderful metaphor for good managers – not the managers on top but those in the center.

What empowerment really means is stopping the disempowering of people

If empowering is about disempowerment, then is decentralization about centralizing? We have confounded our use of these words, too, ever since Alfred P. Sloan, Jr., centralized General Motors in the 1920s in the name of what came to be called decentralization. Recall that Sloan had to rein in a set of businesses that were out of control. There was no decentralization in that.

Part and parcel of this so-called decentralization effort has been the imposition of financial measures – control by the numbers. If division managers met their targets, they were ostensibly free to manage their businesses as they pleased. But the real effect of this decentralization *to* the division head has often been centralization within the division: the concentration of power at the level of the division chief, who is held personally responsible for the impersonal performance.

Division chiefs – and headquarters controllers looking over their shoulders – get very fidgety about surprises and impatient for numerical results. And the best way to ensure quick, expected results is never to do anything interesting; always cut, never create. That is how the rationalization of costs has become to today's manager what bloodletting was to the medieval physician: the cure for every illness.

As a consequence of all this (de)centralizing and (de)layering, measurement has emerged as the religion of management. But how much sensible business behavior has been distorted as people have been pushed to meet the numbers instead of the customers? . . .

The analytical mentality has taken over the field of management. We march to the tune of the technocrat. Everything has to be calculated, explicated, and categorized. The trouble is that technocrats never get much beyond the present. They lack the wisdom to appreciate the past and the imagination to see the future . . . To plan, supposedly to take care of the future, they forecast, which really means they extrapolate current quantifiable trends. (The optimists extrapolate the trends they like, while the pessimists extrapolate ones they don't.) And then, when an unexpected 'discontinuity' occurs (meaning, most likely, that a creative competitor has invented something new), the technocrats run around like so many Chicken Littles, crying, 'The environment's turbulent! The environment's turbulent!'

Measurement is fine for figuring out when to flip a hamburger or how to fill the O.I. bucket at that 'communications' company. But when used to estimate the market for a brand new product or to assess the worth of a complicated professional service, measurement often goes awry. Measurement mesmerizes no less than management. We had better start asking ourselves about the real costs of counting. See 'The soft underbelly of hard data' at the end of this reading.

6. **Great organizations, once created, don't need great leaders**. Organizations that need to be turned around by such leaders will soon turn back again. Go to the popular business press and read just about any article on any company. The whole organization almost always gets reduced to a single individual, the chief at the 'top'. . . . 'CEO Jack Smith didn't just stop the bleeding. With a boost from rising auto sales, he made GM healthy again' (*Fortune*, October 17, 1994). All by himself!

Switzerland is an organization that really works. Yet hardly anybody even knows who's in charge, because seven people rotate in and out of the job of head of state on an annual basis. We may need great visionaries to create great organizations. But after the organizations are created, we don't need heroes, just competent, devoted, and generous leaders who know what's going on and exude that spirit of the hive. Heroes – or, more to the point, our hero worship – reflect nothing more than our own inadequacies. Such worship stops us from thinking for ourselves as adult human beings . . .

Part of this cult of leadership involves an emphasis on the 'turning around' of old, sick companies. Just look what we invest in that! Think of all those consulting firms specializing in geriatrics, ready to help – hardly a pediatric, let alone an obstetric, practice to be found. Why don't we recognize when it's time for an old, sick organization to die? . . .

What we really need, is a kind of Dr. Kevorkian for the world of business – someone to help with pulling the plug. Then young, vibrant companies would get the chance to replace the old, spent ones. Letting more big companies die – celebrating their contributions at grand funerals – would make our societies a lot healthier.

7. **Great organizations have souls; any word with a de or a re in front of it is likely to destroy those souls.** Well, there are still some healthy big organizations out there. You can tell them by their individuality. They stay off the bandwagon, away from the empty fads. Did you ever wonder why so many really interesting ones headquarter themselves far from the chic centers of New York and London? . . .

If you really want to adopt a new technique, don't use its usual name, especially with a *de* or *re*. Call it something completely different. Then you will have to explain it, which means you will have to think about it. You see, techniques are not the problem; just the mindless application of them. Wouldn't it be wonderful if the editors of HBR printed a skull and crossbones next to the title of every article, like those on medicine bottles: an example might be 'Warning! For high-technology companies only; not to be taken by mass-production manufacturers or government agencies.'

Consider the mindless application of reengineering. I opened the popular book on the topic and at first thought. This is not a bad idea. But when I saw the claim on page 2 that the technique 'is to the next revolution of business what specialization of labor was to the last', namely, the Industrial Revolution, I should have closed the book right there. Hype is the problem in management; the medium destroys the message.

Wasn't reengineering what the Ford Motor Company did to automobile production at the turn of the century, what McDonald's did to fast food 30 years ago? Every once in a while, a smart operator comes along and improves a process. Companies like Ford and McDonald's did not need the book; quite the contrary. They needed imagination applied to an intimate knowledge of a business.

In other words, there is no reengineering in the idea of reengineering. Just reification, just the same old notion that the new system will do the job. But because of the hype that goes with any new management fad, everyone has to run around reengineering everything. We are supposed to get superinnovation on demand. Why don't we just stop reengineering and delayering and restructuring and decentralizing and instead start thinking?

8. **It is time to close down conventional M.B.A. programs.** We should be developing real managers, not pretending to create them in the classroom.

I have been doing a survey. I ask people who know a lot about U.S. business to name a few of the really good U.S. chief executives, the leaders who really made, or are making, a major *sustained* difference. I am not talking about the turnaround doctors but the real builders. (Stop here and make your own list.)

You know what? Almost never has anyone been named who has an M.B.A. . . .

Years ago, when things were going better in U.S. business, I used to think that the brilliance of the country's management lay in its action orientation. Managers didn't think a lot; they just got things done. But now I find that the best managers are very thoughtful people who are also highly action oriented. Unfortunately, too many others have stopped thinking. They want quick, easy answers. . . .

It is plain silly to take people who have never been managers – many of whom have not even worked full-time for more than a few years – and pretend to be turning them into managers in a classroom. The whole exercise is too detached from context. We need to stop dumping management theories and cases on people who have no basis even to judge the relevance.

Let's begin by recognizing today's M.B.A. for what it is: technical training for specialized jobs, such as marketing research and financial analysis. (And these are *not* management.) Then maybe we can recognize good management for what *it* is: not some technical profession, certainly not a science or even an applied science (although sometimes the application of science) but a practice, a craft. We have some good things to teach in management schools; let's teach them to people who know what's going on . . .

Now we have a new, insidious track to the executive suite. After the M.B.A., you work as a consultant with some prestigious firm for a time, skipping from one client organization to another. And then you leap straight into the chief executive chair of some company. That system might work on occasion. But it is no way to build a strong corporate sector in society . . .

9. **Organizations need continuous care, not interventionist cures.** That is why nursing is a better model for management than medicine and why women may ultimately make better managers than men. The French term for a medical operation is 'intervention'. Intervening is what all surgeons and too many managers do. Managers keep operating on their systems, radically altering them in the hope of fixing them, usually by cutting things out. Then they leave the consequences of their messy business to the nurses of the corporate world.

Maybe we should try nursing as a model for management. Organizations need to be nurtured – looked after and cared for, steadily and consistently. They don't need to be violated by some dramatic new strategic plan or some gross new reorganization every time a new chief executive happens to parachute in.

In a sense, caring is a more feminine approach to managing, although I have seen it practiced by some excellent male chief executive officers. Still, women do have an advantage, in which case the corporate world is wasting a great deal of talent. Let us, therefore, welcome more women into the executive suites as perhaps our greatest hope for coming to our senses.

A few years ago, I spent a day following around the head nurse of a surgical ward in a hospital. I say 'following around' because she spent almost no time in her office; she was continually on the floor. (Bear in mind that, long ago, the partners of Morgan Stanley operated on the floor, too: their desks were right on the trading floor.) . . .

Off the floor, at the first sign of trouble, empowerment becomes encroachment by senior managers, who, because they don't know what is going on, have no choice but to intervene. And so the organization gets turned into a patient to be cured, even if it was not really sick in the first place. It finds itself alternating between short bouts of radical surgery and long doses of studied inattention.

Consider instead a *craft* style of managing. It is about inspiring, not empowering, about leadership based on mutual respect rooted in common experience and deep understanding. Craft managers get involved deeply enough to know when not to get involved. In contrast to professional managers who claim 'hands off, brain on', the craft manager believes that if there is no laying on of hands, the brain remains shut off.

Women complain about glass ceilings . . . Worse still may be concrete floors. Too many managers can't even see what is going on at the ground level of their organizations, where the products are made and the customers are served (presumably). We need to smash up the ceilings and bust down the floors as well as break through the walls so that people can work together in that one big circle . . .

I guess we have now come full circle, so it is time to conclude with our last musing – about which I will add nothing.

10. **The trouble with today's management is the trouble with this article: everything has to come in short, superficial doses.**

Source: Henry Mintzberg, adapted from 'Musings on Management', *Harvard Business Review*, July–August 1996. Copyright © 1996 by the Harvard Business School Publishing Corporation; all rights reserved.

The soft underbelly of hard data

The belief that strategic managers and their planning systems can be detached from the subject of their efforts is predicated on one fundamental assumption: that they can be informed in a formal way. The messy world of random noise, gossip, inference, impression, and fact must be reduced to firm data, hardened and aggregated so that they can be supplied regularly in digestible form. In other words, systems must do it, whether they go by the name of (reading back over the years) 'information technology', 'strategic information systems', 'expert systems', 'total systems', or just plain so-called 'management information systems' (MIS). Unfortunately, the hard data on which such systems depend often proves to have a decidedly soft underbelly:

1 *Hard information is often limited in scope, lacking richness and often failing to encompass important noneconomic and nonquantitative factors.*

▶

Much information important for strategy making never does become hard fact. The expression on a customer's face, the mood in the factory, the tone of voice of a government official, all of this can be information for the manager but not for the formal system. That is why managers generally spend a great deal of time developing their own *personal* information systems, comprising networks of contacts and informers of all kinds.

2 *Much hard information is too aggregated for effective use in strategy making.* The obvious solution for a manager overloaded with information and pressed for the time necessary to process it is to have the information aggregated. General Electric before 1980 provided an excellent example of this type of thinking. First it introduced 'Strategic Business Units' (SBUs) over the divisions and departments and then 'Sectors' over the SBUs, each time seeking to increase the level of aggregation to enable top management to comprehend the necessary information quickly. The problem is that a great deal is lost in such aggregating, often the essence of the information itself. How much could aggregated data on six sectors really tell the GE chief executives about the complex organization they headed? It is fine to see forests, but only so long as nothing is going on among the trees. As Richard Neustadt, who studied the information-collecting habits of several presidents of the United States, commented: 'It is not information of a general sort that helps a President see personal stakes; not summaries, not surveys, not the *bland amalgams*. Rather . . . it is the odds and ends of *tangible detail* that pieced together in his mind illuminate the underside of issues put before him. . . . He must become his own director of his own central intelligence' (1960:153–154, italics added).

3 *Much hard information arrives too late to be of use in strategy making.* Information takes time to 'harden': time is required for trends and events and performance to appear as 'facts', more time for these facts to be aggregated into reports, even more time if these reports have to be presented on a predetermined schedule. But strategy making has to be an active, dynamic process, often unfolding quickly in reaction to immediate stimuli; managers cannot wait for information to harden while competitors are running off with valued customers.

4 *Finally, a surprising amount of hard information is unreliable.* Soft information is supposed to be unreliable, subject to all kinds of biases. Hard information, in contrast, is supposed to be concrete and precise; it is, after all, transmitted and stored electronically. In fact, hard information can be far worse than soft information. Something is always lost in the process of quantification – before those electrons are activated. Anyone

who has ever produced a quantitative measure – whether a reject count in a factory or a publication count in a university – knows just how much distortion is possible, intentional as well as unintentional. As Eli Devons (1950:Ch. 7) described in his fascinating account of planning for British aircraft production in World War II, despite the 'arbitrary assumptions made' in the collection of some data, 'once a figure was put forward . . . it soon became accepted as the "agreed figure", since no one was able by rational argument to demonstrate that it was wrong . . . And once the figures were called "statistics", they acquired the authority and sanctity of Holy Writ' (155).

Of course, soft information can be speculative, and distorted too. But what marketing manager faced with a choice between today's rumor that a major customer was seen lunching with a competitor and tomorrow's fact that the business was lost would hesitate to act on the former? Moreover, a single story from one disgruntled customer may be worth more than all those reams of market research data simply because, while the latter may identify a problem, it is the former that can suggest the solution. Overall, in our opinion, while hard data may inform the intellect, it is largely soft data that builds wisdom.

References

Devons, E., *Planning in Practice: Essays in Aircraft Planning in War-Time*, Cambridge University Press, 1950.
Neustadt, R. E., *Presidential Power: The Politics of Leadership*, Wiley, 1960.

TO ERR IS HUMAN
BY SPYROS G. MAKRIDAKIS

. . . Wason (1972), a cognitive psychologist, made it his life's goal to learn more about how people search for information and evidence. He found that as much as 90 percent of all the information we are searching for aims at supporting views, beliefs, or hypotheses that we have long cherished. Thus, if a manager thinks that a certain promotional campaign will increase his sales he will look for supportive evidence to prove that the belief (or, more precisely, hypothesis) is correct. Unfortunately, however, it is practically impossible to prove the hypothesis that the promotional campaign is effective simply by observing that sales go up, for there are many factors other than promotions that can cause sales to rise. In this case, supportive evidence can *never* prove the hypothesis is right. That could be done by stopping the promotional campaign for a period of time, the equivalent of getting disconfirming evidence. If the sales then go down, the hypothesis can be proved to be right. If the campaign is stopped several times in several regions, and the outcome is always the same, it can then be ascertained with confidence that the decrease in sales is not due to chance but is influenced by the decrease in advertising. Although it might be impractical to stop promotions or advertising, from a scientific view it is the only way to prove, beyond any reasonable doubt, that the hypothesis that promotions increase sales is correct. People, however, do not look for disconfirming evidence . . .

We tend to remember information that confirms our beliefs far better than information that disproves them

There is another side to the picture. We tend to remember information that confirms our beliefs far better than information that disproves them. In experiments, believers have tended to remember confirming material with 100 percent accuracy, but negative material only about 40 percent of the time. Skeptics, on the other hand, have remembered both supportive and disconfirming evidence equally well – their accuracy was 90 percent in both cases. Thus, not only do we search for supportive evidence, but once we find it we tend to remember it more accurately . . .

The higher up a manager is in the organization, the more the information he or she receives is filtered by several levels of subordinates, as assistants, and secretaries. They know, or think they do, what the manager wants to hear and selectively present supportive information . . .

Can biases be avoided if decisions are made in groups? Unfortunately not – in fact there is evidence suggesting that groups amplify bias by introducing groupthink (a phenomenon that develops when group members become supportive of their leader and each other, thus avoiding conflict and dissent during their meetings) . . .

Another type of judgmental bias that can threaten the effectiveness of decision-making is that of unfounded beliefs or conventional wisdom. We have grown up in a culture where we accept certain statements as true, though they may not be. For instance, we believe that the more information we have, the more accurate our decisions will be. Empirical evidence does not support such a belief. Instead, more information merely seems to increase our confidence that we are right without necessarily improving the accuracy of our decisions . . .

If a manager accepts the human biases I have described in this [article], he cannot assume rationality from his subordinates, superiors, or competitors. This complicates matters considerably, as all economic theories and the vast majority of managerial ones assume cold rationality. How, for instance, does a manager deal with a competitor who is driven by irrational motives? He cannot understand them or predict how they will influence the competitor's decisions. There is no way of doing so, since irrationality cannot be predicted. Thus, another challenge facing managers is to accept the possibility of irrationality and attempt to rationalize it. That is probably the hardest of all challenges a manager must face. Worse, the lack of rationality is not limited to competitors only but exists everywhere. Jealousy, excessive ambition, fighting for no apparent reason, breakdowns in communication, and similar irrational behavior abound in any organization and must be dealt with in a sensible manner in order to neutralize or reduce their negative effects as far as is possible. The challenge is considerable, but it is one that must be confronted. We must move forward, although we know the road will not always be smooth.

Reference

Wason, P.C. and Johnson-Laird P.N., *Psychology of Reasoning: Structure and Content*, Batsford, 1972.

CEOS: SOME GAMBLERS
BY HENRY MINTZBERG

Gambling is a popular metaphor among CEOs, especially in the United States. So let's use this metaphor to consider CEO compensation, since CEOs today gamble in a very particular way.

First, CEO gamblers play with other people's money. That's nice work if you can get it. *Second, CEO gamblers collect, not when they win, but when they seem to be winning.* In CEO gambling, it's never quite clear what will be a winning hand in the end. Never mind: the CEOs collect in the midst of the game. It's like taking in the pot with a couple of aces on the table while the rest of the hand is closed. Poker players call the effort to do this a semi-bluff. CEOs just do it – no semi. The trick, of course, is to make sure the best cards are showing on the table. If the rest of the hand is not great, they can hightail it out of there.

Third, CEO gamblers collect when they have lost too. In other words, they collect as they are hightailing it out of there. This, I assure you, does not happen in real gambling, which has yet to adopt the golden parachute. If it did, imagine the bets those gamblers would make. They'd be 'all in' all the time – the whole pile. Indeed, don't imagine: Check the Chapter 11 records for the bets CEO gamblers have made. In this kind of gambling, wouldn't you be a great 'risktaker' too?

Fourth, CEO gamblers sometimes collect just for drawing cards. No need even to show those aces, or to hightail it out of there (just yet). While CEO gamblers are not always the most resourceful in actively managing their companies, they can be awfully clever in coming up with new ways to collect winnings. For example, some get a bonus for signing a big acquisition, long before anyone can know if it will work out. (Most, by the way, don't.) Not a single card has been turned over, but here comes the cash.

Fifth, CEO gamblers are now able to collect merely for not leaving the table. This is the greatest boondoggle of them all. It's called a 'retention bonus' – you may have heard about it recently. Not only do these CEOs get paid for doing the job (so to speak); they also get paid for not stopping to do the job. Now that is really nice work, if you can get it.

I must point out here that in one respect all of this is like real gambling: the financial payoffs come now, the economic and social consequences trickle in later, after the players have left the table.

If such gambling is so wonderful, shouldn't it be extended to everyone in the company? I believe it must be a mandatory accompaniment of any such CEO compensation package. Especially enthusiastic about this will be the compensation consultants, who must be getting tired of being in bed only with the executives.

Should any board of directors hesitate to embrace this marvelous proposal, I offer another. (When it comes to executive compensation, I suspect that corporate boards are finally ready to take a stand on something – anything.)

This proposal is win–win. Dismiss out of hand, without one second's hesitation, any candidate for a CEO position who seeks a compensation package that would single him or her way out from everyone else in the company. In fact, terminate discussions immediately at the mere mention of the word 'bonus', since this constitutes definitive proof that the candidate has no business running a business of co-operating human beings. (Should this person not comprehend, cite his or her mention a few moments earlier of the importance of 'teamwork', and how 'people are a company's greatest asset'.)

This proposal will save tons of money and send a positive signal to everyone else in the company for a change, while the firm might just end up with a CEO who is a real leader. Imagine that.

One last thing. If the new CEO wishes truly to gamble, point him or her to the nearest casino.

To be sure of hitting the target, shoot first and, whatever you hit, call it the target. Ashleigh Brilliant

CHAPTER 5
MAXIMS OF MANAGING

Dave's Law of Advice: Those with the best advice offer no advice. [Anon]

Maxims are not myths – not quite. (Check your dictionary.) But they can sure lead you down the garden path too. Dave's opening quote of this chapter is just one of many maxims, from A to Z, in our first reading. The second takes us to the grand-daddy of all this management maxim-ising: Parkinson's law. Here Professor C. Northcote Parkinson, with tongue utterly in cheek, explains the mechanics about how 'work expands so as to fill the time available for its completion'.

This takes us into a discussion of a book by Jeffrey Pfeffer and Robert Sutton that challenges management's more popular axioms – about incentive pay, layoffs, mergers and work–life balance.

Lucy Kellaway is great for providing openings and closings to these issues. In this chapter, it's a closing: seven of her own maxims about how to get away with foisting maxims on everyone else.

LAWS AND RULES: FROM A TO Z

Acheson's Rule of the Bureaucracy: A memorandum is written not to inform the reader but to protect the writer.

Berra's Law: You can observe a lot just by watching.

Bonafede's Revelation: The conventional wisdom is that power is an aphrodisiac. In truth, it's exhausting.

Boren's Laws of the Bureaucracy:

1 When in doubt, mumble.

2 When in trouble, delegate.

3 When in charge, ponder.

Cropp's Law: The amount of work done varies inversely with the amount of time spent in the office.

Dave's Law of Advice: Those with the best advice offer no advice.

Dobbins' Law: When in doubt use a bigger hammer.

Principle of Displaced Hassle: To beat the bureaucracy, make your problem their problem.

Dow's Law: In a hierarchical organization, the higher the level, the greater the confusion.

Epstein's Law: If you think the problem is bad now, just wait until we've solved it.

Grossman's Misquote: Complex problems have simple, easy to understand wrong answers.

Heller's Myths of Management: The first myth of management is that it exists. The second myth of management is that success equals skill. Corollary (Johnson): Nobody really knows what is going on anywhere within your organization.

Hendrickson's Law: If a problem causes many meetings, the meetings eventually become more important than the problem.

Hofstadter's Law: It always takes longer than you expect, even when you take into account Hofstadter's Law.

Kettering's Laws: If you want to kill any idea in the world today, get a committee working on it.

The First Myth of Management: It exists.

Maugham's Thought: Only a mediocre person is always at his best.

McGovern's Law: The longer the title, the less important the job.

Pareto's Law (The 20/80 Law): 20% of the customers account for 80% of the turnover, 20% of the components account for 80% of the cost, and so forth.

Parkinson's First Law: Work expands to fill the time available for its completion.

Parkinson's Second Law: Expenditures rise to meet income.

Parkinson's Third Law: Expansion means complexity; and complexity decay.

Parkinson's Fourth Law: The number of people in any working group tends to increase regardless of the amount of work to be done.

Parkinson's Fifth Law: If there is a way to delay an important decision the good bureaucracy, public or private, will find it.

Patton's Law: A good plan today is better than a perfect plan tomorrow.

Peter Principle: In every hierarchy, whether it be government or business, each employee tends to rise to his level of incompetence; every post tends to be filled by an employee incompetent to execute its duties.
Corollaries:

1 Incompetence knows no barriers of time or place.

2 Work is accomplished by those employees who have not yet reached their level of incompetence.

3 If at first you don't succeed, try something else.

Peter's Observation: Super-competence is more objectionable than incompetence.

Pierson's Law: If you're coasting, you're going downhill.

Terman's Law of Innovation: If you want a track team to win the high jump, you find one person who can jump seven feet, not seven people who can jump one foot.

Wolf's Law (An Optimistic View of a Pessimistic World): It isn't that things will necessarily go wrong (Murphy's Law), but rather that they will take so much more time and effort than you think if they are not to go wrong.

Wolf's Law of Decision-Making: Major actions are rarely decided by more than four people. If you think a larger meeting you're attending is really 'hammering out' a decision, you're probably wrong. Either the decision was agreed to by a smaller group before the meeting began, or the outcome of the larger meeting will be modified later when three or four people get together.

Wolf's Law of Management: The tasks to do immediately are the minor ones; otherwise, you'll forget them. The major ones are often better to defer. They usually need more time for reflection. Besides, if you forget them, they'll remind you.

Wolf's Law of Meetings: The only important result of a meeting is agreement about next steps.

Wolf's Law of Planning: A good place to start from is where you are.

Zimmerman's Law: Regardless of whether a mission expands or contracts, administrative overhead continues to grow at a steady rate.

Zimmerman's Law of Complaints: Nobody notices when things go right.

Zusmann's Rule: A successful symposium depends on the ratio of meeting to eating.

Source: Compiled and collected by the authors

PARKINSON'S LAW
BY CYRIL NORTHCOTE PARKINSON

Work expands so as to fill the time available for its completion

General recognition of this fact is shown in the proverbial phrase 'It is the busiest man who has time to spare.' Thus, an elderly lady of leisure can spend the entire day in writing and dispatching a postcard to her niece at Bognor Regis. An hour will be spent finding the postcard, another in hunting for spectacles, half an hour in a search for the address, an hour and a quarter in composition, and twenty minutes in deciding whether or not to take an umbrella when going to the pillar box in the next street. The total effort that would occupy a busy man for three minutes all told may in this fashion leave another person prostrate after a day of doubt, anxiety, and toil.

Granted that work (and especially paperwork) is thus elastic in its demands on time, it is manifest that there need be little or no relationship between the work to be done and the size of the staff to which it may be assigned. A lack of real activity does not, of necessity, result in leisure. A lack of occupation is not necessarily revealed by a manifest idleness. The thing to be done swells in importance and complexity in a direct ratio with the time to be spent. This fact is widely recognized, but less attention has been paid to its wider implications, more especially in the field of public administration. Politicians and taxpayers have assumed (with occasional phases of doubt) that a rising total in the number of civil servants must reflect a growing volume of work to be done. Cynics, in questioning this belief, have imagined that the multiplication of officials must have left some of them idle or all of them able to work for shorter hours. But this is a matter in which faith and doubt seem equally misplaced. The fact is that the number of the officials and the quantity of the work are not related to each other at all. The rise in the total of those employed is governed by Parkinson's Law and would be much the same whether the volume of the work were to increase, diminish, or even disappear. The importance of Parkinson's Law lies in the fact that it is a law of growth based upon an analysis of the factors by which that growth is controlled.

The validity of this recently discovered law must rest mainly on statistical proofs, which will follow. Of more interest to the general reader is the explanation of the factors underlying the general tendency to which this law gives definition. Omitting technicalities (which are numerous) we may distinguish at the outset two motive forces. They can be represented for the present purpose by two almost axiomatic statements, thus: (1) 'An official wants to multiply subordinates, not rivals' and (2) 'Officials make work for each other.'

To comprehend Factor One, we must picture a civil servant, called A, who finds himself overworked. Whether this overwork is real or imaginary is immaterial, but we should observe, in passing, that A's sensation (or illusion) might easily result from his own decreasing energy: a normal symptom of middle age. For this real or imagined overwork there are, broadly speaking, three possible remedies. He may resign; he may ask to halve the work with a colleague called B; he may demand the assistance of two subordinates, to be called C and D. There is probably no instance, however, in history of A choosing any but the third alternative. By resignation he would lose his pension rights. By having B appointed, on his own level in the hierarchy, he would merely bring in a rival for promotion to W's vacancy when W (at long last) retires. So A would rather have C and D, junior men, below him. They will add to his consequence and, by dividing the work into two categories, as between C and D, he will have the merit of being the only man who comprehends them both. It is essential to realize at this point that C and D are, as it were, inseparable. To appoint C alone would have been impossible. Why? Because C, if by himself, would divide the work with A and so assume almost the equal status that has been refused in the first instance to B; a status the more emphasized if C is A's only possible successor. Subordinates must thus number two or more, each being thus kept in order by fear of the other's promotion. When C complains in turn of being overworked (as he certainly will) A will, with the concurrence of C, advise the appointment of two assistants to help C. But he can then avert internal friction only by advising the appointment of two more assistants to help D, whose position is much the same. With this recruitment of E, F, G and H the promotion of A is now practically certain.

there need be little or no relationship between the work to be done and the size of the staff to which it may be assigned

Seven officials are now doing what one did before. This is where Factor Two comes into operation. For these seven make so much work for each other that all are fully occupied and A is actually working harder than ever. An incoming document may well come before each of them in turn. Official E decides that it falls within the province of F, who places a draft reply before C, who amends it drastically before consulting D, who asks G to deal with it. But G goes on leave at this point, handing the file over to H, who drafts a minute that is signed by D and returned to C, who revises his draft accordingly and lays the new version before A.

What does A do? He would have every excuse for signing the thing unread, for he has many other matters on his mind. Knowing now that he is to succeed W next year, he has to decide whether C or D should succeed to his own office. He had to agree to G's going on leave even if not yet strictly entitled to it. He is worried whether H should not have gone instead, for reasons of health. He has looked pale recently – partly but not solely because of his domestic troubles. Then there is the business of F's special increment of salary for the period of the conference and E's application for transfer to the Ministry of Pensions. A has heard that D is in love with a married typist and that G and F are no longer on speaking terms – no-one seems to know why. So A might be tempted to sign C's draft and have done with it. But A is a conscientious man. Beset as he is with problems created by his colleagues for themselves and for him – created by the mere fact of these officials' existence – he is not the man to shirk his duty. He reads through the draft with care, deletes the fussy paragraphs added by C and H, and restores the thing to the form preferred in the first instance by the able (if quarrelsome) F. He corrects the English – none of these young men can write grammatically – and finally produces the same reply he would have written if officials C to H had never been born. Far more people have taken far longer to produce the same result. No-one has been idle. All have done their best. And it is late in the evening before A finally quits his office and begins the return journey to Ealing. The last of the office lights are being turned off in the gathering dusk that marks the end of another day's administrative toil. Among the last to leave, A reflects with bowed shoulders and a wry smile that late hours, like grey hairs, are among the penalties of success.

Source: C. Northcote Parkinson, *Parkinson's Law: The Pursuit of Progress*, John Murray, 1958. Reprinted by permission of John Murray (Publishers) Limited.

MAXIMS IN NEED OF A MAKEOVER
BY JUSTIN EWERS

To many, they are the commandments of business management – truths to be ignored at a company's peril. Say them together now: Great leaders make great companies. Strategy is destiny. Change or die.

But here's a thought: What if some of the business world's most dearly held

> ## What if some of the business world's most dearly held axioms are wrong?
> ## What if there is a better way?

axioms are wrong? What if there is a better way? This is the argument Jeffrey Pfeffer and Robert Sutton, management professors at Stanford University, make in their new book, out this week, *Hard Facts, Dangerous Half-Truths, and Total Nonsense: Profiting From Evidence-Based Management.* Gathering the work of psychologists, sociologists, and management experts, the authors make a compelling case that some of business's beloved truths are far from self-evident. Too many business leaders, they argue, are making decisions based on vague hunches, management fads, and heroic-success stories instead of on empirical data. Too often, the consequences are grave. 'If doctors practiced medicine the way many companies practice management,' Pfeffer and Sutton write, 'there would be far more sick and dead patients, and many more doctors would be in jail.'

More than a few management experts agree that some of these Olde Business Maxims are long overdue for a makeover. 'They have really touched a nerve here,' says Tom Donaldson, a professor of ethics at the University of Pennsylvania's Wharton School of Business: 'Managers often don't know what they don't know.' So what is a Jack Welch disciple to do? *U.S. News* sat down with Pfeffer and Sutton to discuss their five favorite myths of management – and to see who they think is practicing business their way.

Myth 1. Financial incentives drive good performance

Managers often think money can solve all their problems. Workers not performing the way you'd like them to? Tie their pay to performance. Executives haven't bought into the company's mission? Offer them stock options. Pfeffer and Sutton argue, though, that using financial incentives to improve performance isn't quite so simple.

Too many managers overlook the fact that incentives can inspire bad behavior as well as good – and often hurt performance as much as they help it. Take the incentive system put in place recently by the city of Albuquerque, N.M. To cut down on overtime paid to garbage truck drivers, the city began to encourage workers to finish their routes on time or early, by offering a driver who completed a route in five hours, say, three additional hours of 'incentive pay'. The results were not quite what the city had hoped. Drivers drove too fast, often in trucks that were overweight, and in many cases garbage didn't even get picked up. 'When you tie money to incentives, people will not necessarily focus on what's best for the organization,' says Sutton. 'They'll focus on what it takes to get the incentive.'

Which, of course, can lead down a slippery ethical slope. In a study conducted last year comparing 435 companies that restated their earnings with those that did not, researchers at the University of Minnesota found that the bigger the proportion of stock options in senior executives' payment packages, the more likely the companies were to have to restate their finances. Cooking the books, in other words, became increasingly tempting the more salary was linked to stock price.

So why do so many companies keep trying it? Simple intellectual inertia, says Pfeffer: At some point, 'it just becomes what everybody does; nobody thinks about it anymore. They don't ask if it's appropriate, if it fits their particular circumstances. They don't ask anything – they just do it.' Managers don't seem to realize that equity incentives rarely improve company performance. But they should. 'The lesson here,' the authors write, 'is a variant on an old adage: Be careful what you pay for, you may actually get it.'

Myth 2. First-movers have the advantage

There is something about this idea that appeals to the entrepreneur in every executive: Be the first to move into a market, and you'll have it all to yourself. Victory will be yours.

But actually, it may be better for a business in the long run to be second or even third. 'Success stories that support first-mover [advantage] turn out to be false,' says Sutton. 'People believe in it religiously, but the evidence is mixed.' There are plenty of infamous first-movers, after all, that did *not* go on to dominate their markets: Xerox invented the first PC, Netscape came up with the Internet browser, Ampex produced the first VCR – and yet none of these companies managed to hold on to their leads. Meanwhile, Microsoft has made a living coming in second: Windows is a copy of the Mac; Excel followed Lotus 1-2-3; Internet Explorer jumped into water warmed by Netscape. And Bill Gates isn't alone. Wal-Mart was hardly the first discount retailer. Apple wasn't the first company to sell MP3 players. And Amazon wasn't the first to sell books online. 'At first blush, it sounds like a good idea,' says Sutton, 'but as soon as you start challenging assumptions, it's a half-truth.'

Many other management experts concur. 'We're still looking for the silver bullet: "If you do this, you will guarantee success; if you do that, you'll guarantee failure,"' says Barry Staw, a professor of leadership and communication at the University of California-Berkeley's Haas School of Business. But being first to move into a market is not necessarily it. 'A lot of what's effective management is doing things well and doing it over and over again,' says Sutton. Too many managers become obsessed with being first, when coming in second, oddly enough, may be the most cost-effective way to be the best.

Myth 3. Layoffs are a good way to cut costs

It seems like basic economics. If you have a company with 100 employees, and you're over budget by 10 percent, laying off 10 workers will solve your problem. In one stroke, there go hundreds of thousands of dollars in salaries, healthcare benefits, and 401(k) plans – and suddenly your balance sheet is looking much better.

Not so fast, say Pfeffer and Sutton. While some research shows that layoffs have no effect on long-term financial performance, and other data show they have a negative effect, there are few studies, if any, demonstrating that layoffs have a positive effect on company performance. A recent report by Bain & Co., in fact, found companies that manage to avoid layoffs – even in tough financial straits – end up better off financially in the long term.

Witness the recent successes of SAS Institute, the world's largest privately owned software company, and Xilinx, a maker of computer chips. Both companies struggled mightily through the dot-bomb crisis with the same slumping growth as their competitors, but they avoided layoffs – and the loss of service, product innovation, and development that often come with them.

The result: 'SAS made a killing in the middle of the downturn,' says Pfeffer, by attracting customers frustrated with the dwindling services offered by their competitors. In 2005, Xilinx was named the No.1 high-tech company to work for by *Fortune* magazine. Both companies successfully weathered the recession and are still hiring.

Too many managers have itchy trigger fingers when it comes to layoffs. In one survey of 720 companies conducted by the American Management Association, 30 percent said they'd been forced to hire back people they'd laid off or to use them as contractors. Sometimes, of course, layoffs can't be avoided, but before managers take such a drastic, morale-destroying step, they should consider the myriad other, cheaper ways to cut costs – trimming travel budgets, say, or executive pay. Believe it or not, it might even save them money.

Myth 4. Mergers are a good idea

It is no secret that the vast majority of mergers fail to deliver their intended benefits – about 70 percent, according to some estimates. What's incredible, though, are the sheer numbers of executives who keep trying them anyway. 'Everybody says they know the data but it's not going to happen to us,' says Pfeffer. The bankers come knocking, the PowerPoints go up, the smell of blood is in the water, and companies close their eyes and take their leaps of faith. 'If a doctor tells you that 70 percent of the time this is going to make things worse instead of better, and people keep doing it anyway, well, that's crazy,' says Sutton.

Most mergers fail to live up to expectations for one of three reasons: The companies are too similar in size (DaimlerChrysler), they are too geographically distant (SynOptics and Wellfleet Communications), or their cultural differences run too deep (AOL-TimeWarner). Hewlett-Packard's merger with Compaq in 2001 is an example of the perfect storm: Two companies of roughly equal size, one in Silicon Valley and one in Houston, struggled mightily with their fundamentally different cultures. (One example: HP employees used voice mail to communicate; Compaq used E-mail. 'So they literally couldn't talk to each other,' says Sutton.) The result? A tailspin that resulted last year in the ousting of CEO Carly Fiorina.

Still, there are a few companies, like Cisco Systems, for example, that seem to be exceptions to this merger rule. Since 1993, Cisco has acquired a total of 108 companies without a major hiccup. Its secret? Senior managers have looked at what went right and wrong in other companies' mergers – and used the evidence to their benefit. They have avoided the pull of the big deal, focusing instead on smaller, targeted acquisitions. They have learned to trust their instincts: 'When you're going through the negotiation process, it's like dating,' says Dan Scheinman, the company's senior vice president of corporate development. 'If you don't like someone you're dating, getting married doesn't solve the problem.' Most important, the company practices what it preaches: 'A lot of companies treat [mergers] as an event: "We did it;

we've got the press conference; we're done,"' he says. 'For us, we've got the acquisition, then the next step, then the next.' Evidence-based management seems to work: Nearly half of the 10,000 employees Cisco has acquired in the past 12 years have stayed with the company.

Myth 5. Life and work should be kept separate

It is a truism that dominates almost every office building in the country. Intraoffice dating and marriage are no-nos. Jobs aren't offered to people who 'smile too much'. Senior partners frown on dogs or kids in the office. 'You should consider your coworker your enemy,' former CEO James Halpin of CompUSA once told his employees.

But wait. Why are businesses so determined to keep work and life separate? There is certainly plenty of evidence that companies willing to gray the line between work and play aren't suffering as a result. Google, for example, asks employees to spend 70 percent of their time on the company's core business, then gives workers the remaining 30 percent to work on other projects related to new business – something akin to what they would do for fun. Does it work? The proof may be in the pudding. Out of this 'free time' Google News, Google Earth, and Google Local have emerged.

Southwest Airlines has gone a step further – tossing the old maxim about intraoffice relationships to the wind. About 2,200 of the 32,000 employees at the company are married to someone at Southwest. 'We've talked to our employees from Day 1 about being one big family,' Colleen Barrett, the company's president, told the authors. 'If you stop and think about it for even 20 seconds, the things we do are things you would do with your own family.' Southwest sends birthday cards and letters of congratulation on the anniversary of each employee's hire. The company acknowledges when employees' children are sick or when there has been a death in the family. And the message seems to be getting through: One study of the major carriers in the U.S. airline industry found that Southwest employees did, in fact, talk about the company as if it were an extension of their family. They use 'we' to describe their employer. Southwest attracts 30 or more applicants for every job opening. Driving a wedge between work and life is a fool's errand, says Pfeffer. 'The idea that you can separate those two is just impossible.' The more companies that realize it, the sooner *work* won't have to be a four-letter word.

Source: Justin Ewers, *U.S. News and World Report*, 19 March 2006. Copyright 2006 *U.S. News and World Report*, L.P. Reprinted with permission.

WHY MOST MANAGERS ARE PLAGIARISTS
BY LUCY KELLAWAY

A few years ago, William Swanson, head of the world's biggest missile maker, sat down to write a little book containing the secrets of his greatness.

There is nothing unusual about this. Most chief executives like to dispense potted wisdom, and many think their aphorisms worthy of publication. Mr Swanson's rules, of which there were 33, were slightly above average for this lamentable literary genre. The content was the usual mixture of platitude, wishful thinking and plain dullness but the style was lucid enough, and the jargon content low.

To give you a flavour – rule 32: do not ever lose your sense of humour. This is clear, though tedious and unhelpful. Moreover, one suspects Mr Swanson did not follow it himself as putting out a collection of maxims shows one's sense of humour has been lost long ago.

His company, Raytheon, distributed more than one-quarter of a million copies of *Unwritten Rules of Management* and the great Warren Buffett apparently liked it enough to request a couple of dozen extras.

The story would have ended on this happy, if somewhat uneventful, note were it not for a young engineer who spotted that 17 of the rules bore an uncanny resemblance to a book called *The Unwritten Laws of Engineering* published in 1944 by W.J. King. The young man wrote this up in his blog. From there, the story made it into newspapers.

Mr Swanson squirmed a bit and tried to laugh it off, but last week was told by his board that he had erred and was to be punished by forgoing his pay rise for the year. However, they said they still considered him to be a terrific leader and declared he could continue with his job regardless. Red face, small slap, but otherwise business as usual.

So what do we learn from this odd tale? I dare say there are at least 33 managerial maxims that this touches, but observing rule six (below), I'm going to limit mine to seven.

1 *There are no new management rules under the sun.* Peter Drucker said most that was worth saying on how to manage a long time ago. Since then it has all been endless repetition. If a CEO's maxims are true they are bound to have been said before, often.

2 *Management itself is about plagiarism.* This is the first great rule that anyone serious about making it as a manager must learn: make sure you take the credit for other people's actions and ideas. Not all of it perhaps, but a healthy slug. Given this basic fact of management life, Mr Swanson's crime looks rather less serious. Copying out someone's words seems less grave than routinely passing off your colleagues' ideas as your own, as most managers do without thinking, every day.

3 *An exception to rule one. If you have made a mistake, reverse plagiarism kicks in.* The secret now is to try to make someone else the author of what you have done. This can be hard, and Mr Swanson failed horribly. When the New York Times challenged him with his copying habit, he said he had given the 1944 book and his notes to a staff member to write the presentation, so he had no idea how much of it was not his own words. Which is lame, even as lame excuses go.

4 *If you wish to copy out someone else's work, change the word order around a bit*. King wrote: 'Be extremely careful of the accuracy of your statements.' There were surely other ways of getting across the same – unremarkable – view. But this is the phrasing that Mr Swanson plumped for: 'Be extremely careful of the accuracy of your statements.'

5 *If you have ignored rule four and got caught copying out of management books, do not give the standard excuse*, as Mr Swanson did, that he had absorbed the material unconsciously through a lifetime's reading. This does not wash at all. I have read dozens of management books in my life, and cannot recall a single thing from any of them.

6 *If you insist on listing maxims, 33 is far too many*. Ten were enough for God, but seven is better still.

7 *Boards should not sit on fences*. Sack me or back me is surely the nature of these things. If the Raytheon board considered him to have done something badly wrong (which I do not think he did, in the scheme of things) they should have sacked him. Otherwise he should have blushed, apologised and moved on.

looking an absolute idiot is not the thing if you are trying to be a business leader

And now for a principle I have plagiarised from the *New York Times*: *fat cats get off scot free yet again*. Kaavya Viswanathan, the 19-year-old Harvard student whose much-hyped novel contained large chunks copied out of other books, has become a national villain and her writing career is ruined. Meanwhile, 57-year-old Mr Swanson, who is responsible for 80,000 employees and to the military who use his kit, has shown his integrity to be gravely wanting but has been allowed to carry on regardless.

I do not accept this. What he did was less serious than what she did. Novels are meant to be fresh – that is the point of them. We know business leaders talk a lot of guff. Whether it is their own guff or someone else's seems not terribly important.

In the booklet, Mr Swanson expressed the hope that after reading it 'maybe you too can become a leader of a company'. In the – frankly inconceivable – case that anyone was helped in this way, I hope this little story may have taught them something even more useful. Writing a book of maxims is an exercise in vanity and a hostage to fortune. The real upshot is that Swanson now looks an idiot.

Which leads me to my final, breathtakingly obvious maxim: *looking an absolute idiot is not the thing if you are trying to be a business leader*.

Source: Lucy Kellaway, FT.com, 7 May 2006.

The mainstream is a current too strong to think in. Paul Shepheard, in What is Architecture

CHAPTER 6
MASTERS OF MANAGING?

Education, n. 'That which discloses to the wise and disguises from the foolish their lack of understanding.' [Ambrose Bierce, The Devil's Dictionary, 1906]

If there is a message to all of the above, it is that management is a practice, learned in context. No manager, let alone leader, has ever been created in a classroom. With this in mind, Chapter 6 takes a close look at 'management' 'education'.

Who are the 'masters of managing'? Some excuse for education. MBA programmes are not much better, argues Henry Mintzberg in excerpts from his book Managers not MBAs: *about Jack's turn in an apocryphal Harvard case study classroom; with a list of some rather worrying impressions left by MBA education; some surprising data about the performance of Harvard's best CEOs; and, to wrap it all up, the comparison of an MBA student who dropped in to his office, with someone who came in to clean the bugs out of the light fixtures. Guess who shed more light on management.*

Philip Broughton, as a recent MBA, has shed considerable light on his compatriots in this topsy-turvy economy. So does Andrew Policano, in a comment about the rating games played by his fellow MBA deans. The latter sounds like the numbers games played by CEOs – in spite of all those new courses on ethics. So maybe it's time to educate for real.

MANAGERS NOT MBAs
BY HENRY MINTZBERG

Jack's turn

*[In lecture courses, students] are waiting for you to give 'the answer' . . .
What we say with the case method is 'Look, I know you don't have enough
information – but given the information you do have, what are you going
to do?'*[1]

'Ok Jack, here you are at Matsushita: what are you going to do now?' The
professor and eighty-seven of Jack's classmates anxiously await his reply to
the cold call. Jack is prepared; he has thought about this for a long time,
ever since he was told that the case study method is supposed to 'challenge
conventional thinking'. He has also been told repeatedly that good managers
are decisive, therefore good MBA students have to take a stand. So Jack
swallows hard and answers.

'How can I answer that question?' Jack begins. 'I barely heard of Matsushita
before yesterday. Yet today you want me to pronounce on its strategy.'

'Last night, I had two other cases to prepare. So Matsushita, with its
hundreds of thousands of employees and thousands of products, got a couple
of hours. I read the case over once quickly and again, let's say, less quickly.
I never knowingly used any of its products. (I didn't even know before
yesterday that Matsushita makes Panasonic.) I never went inside any of their
factories. I've never even been to Japan. I spoke to none of their customers.
I certainly never met any of the people mentioned in the case. Besides, this is
a pretty high-tech issue and I'm a pretty low-tech guy. My work experience,
such as it was, took place in a furniture factory. All I have to go on are these
twenty pages. This is a superficial exercise. I refuse to answer your question!'

What happens to Jack? I'll let you guess. But from there, he goes back
to the furniture business, where he immerses himself in its products and
processes, the people and the industry. He is an especially big fan of
its history. Gradually, with his courage to be decisive and to challenge
conventional thinking, Jack rises to become CEO. There, with hardly any
industry analysis at all (that would have come in a later course), he crafts a
strategy that changes the industry.

Meanwhile, Bill, sitting next to Jack, leaps in. He has never been to Japan
either (although he did know that Matsushita makes Panasonic). Bill makes a
clever point or two, and gets that MBA. That gets him a job in a prestigious
consulting firm, where, like those cases study classes, he goes from one
situation to another, each time making a clever point or two, concerning
issues he recently knew nothing about, always leaving before implementation
begins. As this kind of experience pours in, it is not long before Bill becomes
chief executive of a major appliance company. (He never consulted for one,

but it does remind him of that Matsushita case.) There he formulates a fancy high-tech strategy, which is implemented through a dramatic program of acquisitions. What happens to that? Guess again.

> *Readers [of Kelly and Kelly's book,* What They Really Teach You at the Harvard Business School] *are probably asking – read the case and do that analysis in two to four hours? Harvard's answer is yes. Students need to prepare two to three cases each day . . . So [they] must work toward getting their analysis done fast as well as done well.*[2]

The impression left by MBA education

1 Managers are important people who sit above others, disconnected from the work of making products and selling services. The higher 'up' these managers go, the more important they become. At the 'top' sits the chief executive who *is* the corporation (even if he or she only arrived yesterday).

2 Managing is decision making based on systematic analysis. To manage, therefore, is to deem. It is more science than art, with no mention of craft.

3 The data for such decision making comes from brief convenient packages of words and numbers, called cases in school and reports in practice. To make decisions, the numbers are 'massaged' and the words are debated, perhaps with some added consideration of 'ethics'.

4 Under these managers sit their organizations, neatly separated like MBA programs into the functions of finance, marketing, accounting, etc., each of which applies its own repertoire of techniques.

5 To bring these functions together, managers pronounce 'strategies', which are very special and, however mysterious, can be understood by people who have been taught industry analysis and given the opportunity to formulate many of them in a case study classroom.

6 The best strategies are clear, simple, deliberate, and bold, like those of the heroic leaders of the most interesting case studies.

7 After these MBA managers have finished formulating their strategies, all the other people – known as 'human resources' – must scurry around implementing them. Implementation is important because it is about the taking of action, which managers must control but never do.

8 This implementation is, however, no easy matter, because while the managers who have been to business school embrace change, many of those human resources resist it. So these managers have to 'bash bureaucracy', by the use of formulaic techniques, and then to 'empower' whoever is left to do the work they have been hired to do. This no manager must ever change.

9 To become such a manager, better still a 'leader' who gets to sit on top of everyone else, you must first sit still for two years in a business school. That enables you to manage anything.

The performance of Harvard's best

In the early 2000s, I came across David Ewing's book entitled *Inside the Harvard Business School*, which was published in 1990. Ewing saw himself as just the person to write such a book, since he had 'seen the school from the inside out for four decades, personally known most of its leaders, taught, and had a hand in many of its struggles'. So, from an 'insider's viewpoint', he set out 'to answer such questions [as why the school "has become" so "important"]' (p. 7).

Early in the book (pp. 4–5), Ewing presented his list of Harvard alumni who 'had made it to the top' in business – 19 people in all, Harvard's superstars presumably. A biased sample if ever there was one. So we decided to use it as such. (Joe Lampel joined me in the analysis.)

We had the advantage of hindsight: more than a decade had passed since the list was published . . . 'the real test of the [Harvard Business School] is . . . how its alumni perform,' Ewing wrote (p. 274). How, then, did Harvard's presumably best alumni perform, not in getting there but in managing there?

In a word, badly. Looking at the record as of late 2003 . . . ten of the nineteen seem clearly to have failed (meaning that the company went bankrupt, they were forced out of the CEO chair, a major merger backfired, etc.). The performance of another four could be called questionable at least. Some of these fourteen CEOs built up or turned around businesses, prominently and dramatically, only to see them weaken or collapse dramatically. None of the fourteen left behind a solid sustainable business.

Joe Lampel noted an often fatal tendency to pursue a formula – some kind of generic technique – in disregard of nuance and in spite of people and execution problems. Inexperienced students who seek 'practical' applications in the classroom seem to become disconnected managers who seek easy answers on the job.

So what do we conclude from this? Not that the MBA is a dysfunctional degree that ruins everyone who gets it. There are graduates of these programs who are doing fine, just as there are those with the degree who have failed miserably. The evidence presented here is not definitive. But it should make us all highly suspicious about this influential degree. Having an MBA should no more qualify people to manage than it should disqualify them. But the data provided above should certainly sound some warning bells: that the MBA confers important advantages on many of the wrong people. Put differently, people should be earning their managerial stripes on the job; that process should not be speeded up in any classroom. No company should tolerate the 'fast track'.

The MBA and the bug cleaner

I was sitting in my office at the Insead business school near Paris a few years back when I received two knocks on my door, a couple of weeks apart. The first was from an MBA student about to complete his studies. He wanted to know about Bombardier, the high flying Canadian company. He had heard good things about it and considered writing for a job there. Was it as good as they say, he wanted to know, and did I think it would sustain its success for 'another ten or fifteen years'? (Another MBA risk taker!)

How was I to know, I answered. They are certainly doing well now. But who knows what will happen after the guy who built up the place retires, or if it runs into some problem with one of its planes. (Later he did retire. And it ran into problems with one of its trains.) Besides, I asked, why should they hire you? Have you had any experience in their fields of aircraft, transportation equipment, sports vehicles? Just because you have an MBA?

I am sure he found a good job, if not with Bombardier, then with some other company that was happy to have his experience, whatever it was.

A couple of weeks later, the knock was very different. It came from a maintenance man, sent to clean the bugs out of my fluorescent lights. He was a talkative fellow, and well informed about the things he wanted to discuss. He read all kinds of OECD documents, he told me, and was worried about many of the trends he saw. 'When I first started to work, we worked as a team. There was a boss, of course, but he was the best informed; his job was to train the younger people.' Now all of that has changed, he bemoaned; titles and status have taken over. The bosses often don't know what's going on. The old kind of leadership, which respected the workers and knew the work, was better. He was concerned that society was moving into a dangerous state.

When he left, he thanked me, saying that he felt much better for having discussed this. I thanked him too. So did I, I replied, although I doubt he realized how much!

Here we have two very different views of leadership in society. Which would you choose? We do have a choice.

Reference

Ewing, D.W., *Inside the Harvard Business School: Strategies and Lessons of America's Leading School of Business*, Times Books, 1990.

Footnotes

1 Lieber (1999), quoting Roger Martin, 'Learning and change', *Fast Company*, 30, 262.
2 Kelly, F. and Kelly, H.M., *What They Really Teach You at the Harvard Business School*, Warner, 1986: 46.

Source: Excerpted from Henry Mintzberg, *Managers Not MBAs*, FT/Prentice Hall, 2004.

HARVARD'S MASTERS OF THE APOCALYPSE
BY PHILIP DELVES BROUGHTON

If his fellow Harvard MBAs are all so clever, how come so many are now in disgrace?

If Robespierre were to ascend from hell and seek out today's guillotine fodder, he might start with a list of those with three incriminating initials beside their names: MBA. The Masters of Business Administration, that swollen class of jargon-spewing, value-destroying financiers and consultants have done more than any other group of people to create the economic misery we find ourselves in.

From Royal Bank of Scotland to Merrill Lynch, from HBOS to Lehman Brothers, the Masters of Disaster have their fingerprints on every recent financial fiasco.

I write as the holder of an MBA from Harvard Business School – once regarded as a golden ticket to riches, but these days more like scarlet letters of shame. We MBAs are haunted by the thought that the tag really stands for Mediocre. But Arrogant, Mighty Big Attitude, Me Before Anyone and Management By Accident. For today's purposes, perhaps it should be Masters of the Business Apocalypse.

Harvard Business School alumni include Stan O'Neal and John Thain, the last two heads of Merrill Lynch, plus Andy Hornby, former chief executive of HBOS, who graduated top of his class. And then of course, there's George W. Bush, Hank Paulson, the former US Treasury secretary, and Christopher Cox, the former chairman of the Securities and Exchange Commission (SEC), a remarkable trinity who more than fulfilled the mission of their alma mater: 'To educate leaders who make a difference in the world.'

It just wasn't the difference the school had hoped for.

Business schools have shown a remarkable ability to miss the economic catastrophes unfolding before their eyes.

In the late 1990s, their faculties rushed to write paeans to Enron, the firm of the future, the new economic paradigm. The admiration was mutual: Enron was stuffed with Harvard Business School alumni, from Jeff Skilling, the chief executive, down. When Enron, rotten to the core, collapsed, the old case studies were thrust in a closet and removed from the syllabus, and new ones were promptly written about the ethical and accounting issues posed by Enron's misadventures.

Much the same appears to have happened with Royal Bank of Scotland.

When I was a student at Harvard Business School, between 2004 and 2006, I recall a distinguished professor of organisational behaviour, Joel Podolny, telling us proudly of his work with Fred Goodwin at RBS. At the time, RBS looked like a corporate supermodel and Podolny was keen to trumpet his role in its transformation. A Harvard Business School case study of the firm entitled The Royal Bank of Scotland: Masters of Integration, written in 2003, began with a quote from the man we now know as Fred the Shred or the World's Worst Banker: 'Hard work, focus, discipline and concentrating on what our customers need. It's quite a simple formula really, but we've just been very, very consistent with it.'

The authors of the case, two Harvard Business School professors, described the 'new architecture' formed by RBS after its acquisition of NatWest, the clusters of customer-facing units, the successful 'buy-in' by employees. Goodwin came across as a management master, saying: 'A leader's job is to create the conditions that enable people to believe, in their hearts and minds, in the value of what they are doing.'

Then just last December, Harvard Business School revised and republished another homage to RBS – The Royal Bank of Scotland Group: The Human Capital Strategy.

It is tragic to read now of all the effort put in by those under Goodwin, from 'pulse surveys' to track employee performance to 'the big thank you', a website where managers could recognise individual excellence in customer service.

Every trendy business school idea was being implemented, it seemed, while what really mattered – the bank's risk assessment, cash flow and capital structure – was going to hell. To be fair, neither Podolny nor the authors of the case studies were finance professors, but it's still pretty shocking that a school that purports to teach general management should fail to see the gaping problems at a firm they studied in such depth.

Is there a pattern here? Go back to the 1980s, and you find that Harvard MBAs played a big enough role in the insider trading scandals that washed through Wall Street for a former chairman of the SEC to consider it a good move to donate millions of dollars for the teaching of ethics at the school.

Time after time, and scandal after scandal, it seems that a school that graduates just 900 students a year finds itself in the thick of it. Yet there is remarkably little contrition.

Last October, Harvard Business School celebrated its 100th birthday with a global summit in Boston. While Wall Street and Washington descended into an economic inferno, Jay Light, the dean of the school and a board member at the Black-stone private equity group, opened the festivities by shrugging off any responsibility.

'We all failed to understand how much [the financial system] had changed in the past 15 years or so, and how fragile it might be because of increased leverage, decreased transparency and decreased liquidity: three of the crucial things in the world of financial markets,' he said.

'We all failed to understand how that fragility could evidence itself in a frozen short-term credit system, something that hadn't really happened since 1907. We also probably overestimated the ability of the political process to deal with the realities of what could happen if real trouble developed.

'What we have witnessed is a stunning and sobering failure of financial safeguards, of financial markets, of financial institutions and mostly of leadership at many levels. We will leave the talk of fixing the blame to others. That is not very interesting. But we must be involved in fact in fixing the problem.'

You would think after failing on so many levels, the school that provides more business leaders than any other might feel some remorse. Not in the least. It's onwards and upwards, with the very people who blew apart the world's financial plumbing now demanding to fix the leak.

You can draw up a list of the greatest entrepreneurs of recent history, from Larry Page and Sergey Brin of Google and Bill Gates of Microsoft, to Michael Dell, Richard Branson, Lakshmi Mittal – and there's not an MBA between them.

Yet the MBA industry continues to grow, and business schools provide vital income to academic institutions: 500,000 people around the world now graduate each year with an MBA, 150,000 of those in the United States, creating their own management class within global business.

Given the present chaos, shouldn't we be asking if business education is not just a waste of time, but actually damaging to our economic health?

Shouldn't we be asking if business education is not just a waste of time, but actually damaging to our economic health?

If doctors or lawyers wreaked such havoc in their own professions, we would certainly reconsider what is being taught at medical and law schools.

During my time at the school, 50 students were chosen to participate in a detailed survey of their development. Scott Snook, the professor who ran it, reported that about a third of students were inclined to define right and wrong simply in terms of what everyone else was doing.

'They can't really step back and take a critical view,' he said. 'They're totally defined by others and by the outcomes of what they're doing.'

A group of people unable to see their actions in the broader context of the society they inhabit have no business being self-regulating. Yet in the financial services industry this is pretty much what they demanded and to a large extent got – with catastrophic consequences.

The happiest in my cohort, which graduated into the rosy economic conditions of 2006, are now certainly those who went off to do the unfashionable jobs: a friend who spurned Wall Street to join a Mid-western industrial firm, and now finds himself running the agricultural division of an Indian conglomerate; one who joined a foundation promoting entrepreneurship; one who went into Boston city government, another who moved to Russia to run a cinema chain.

However, these were the rarities: 42% of my class went into financial services and another 21% into consulting, both wretched sectors to be in today and for the foreseeable future.

Applications to business schools in America and Europe are broadly up, as people search for a safe haven from the recession. What are they thinking? Many MBA jobs will not be coming back. Students who stump up more than £60,000 for a two-year MBA can expect a long wait to make that back.

For those about to graduate from business school, these are grim times. Financial and consulting firms, which used to soak up two-thirds of the MBAs from top schools, have all but vanished from campuses. Suddenly jobs in government and at nonprofit organisations are in hot demand from students who used to consider them laughably underpaid.

A dose of modesty among MBAs and business schools is long overdue. But it's not going to come from Harvard. Light, told his audience in October: 'The need for leadership in the world today is at least as great as it has ever been. The need for what we do is at least as great as it has ever been.'

A bold claim to which many might say: please, spare us.

Source: 'If his fellow Harvard MBAs are so clever, how come so many are now in disgrace?', Philip Delves Broughton, *The Sunday Times*, 1 March 2009. © The Times 1 March 2009/nisyndication.com.

GAMES BUSINESS SCHOOLS PLAY
BY ANDREW J. POLICANO

If your MBA program is in the unenviable group that *Business Week* and *U.S. News & World Report* rank below the top 25, you are undoubtedly under constant pressure from your students, alumni, and donors to move into the top 25. The following . . . steps [among others] can get you there . . .

- *Provide a wide variety of students' services for MBA students*, including free breakfasts and luncheons . . . and free parking . . .

- *Increase the average GMAT score of your MBA class to above 650* . . . You will need to decrease the number of students in the MBA program . . . and never admit students who have low GMAT scores, even if they otherwise show strong potential . . .

- *Increase services to recruiters*, including valet parking, free meals, gift baskets in hotel rooms, and a comfortable lounge area . . .

- *Eliminate not-for-profit programs and other MBA majors that produce graduates who are placed in low-salary positions* . . .

- *Entice everyone who inquires about [your] program, especially unqualified students, to apply* . . . (U.S. News uses the number of admits divided by the number of applicants as a selectivity measure.) . . .

- *Increase the budget for the MBA program substantially; $50,000 per student is a good target* . . . you will need to reallocate funds . . . [for example, by decreasing] the size and/or the cost of delivery of your undergraduate [and doctoral] program[s] [and diverting] resources from the support of faculty research to the MBA programs . . .

If you think that these suggestions seem tongue-in-cheek, think again. They are only a fraction of what many deans over the years have described to me as their 'rankings strategy'.

Source: Excerpted from Andrew J. Policano, *Ten Easy Steps to a Top-25 MBA Program*, *Selections*: The Magazine of the Graduate Management Admission Council, 1, no. 2 (2001): 39–40.

To be good is noble, but to teach others how to be good is nobler – and less trouble. Mark Twain

CHAPTER 7
METAMORPHOSING MANAGEMENT

Only the very wisest and the very stupidest never change. [Confucius]

There is an enormous literature and consulting practice aimed at helping managers deal with major changes in their organisations – turnaround, revitalisation, downsizing, etc. Most of this is about 'managed change'. Be careful: the point can well be made – done articulately in our first reading, by Jim Clemmer – that this term is an oxymoron. Change should not be 'managed', he suggests, at least when this word is used to mean forced, made to happen. Maybe the best way to 'manage' change is to just let it happen – to set up the conditions whereby people will follow their natural instincts to experiment and transform behaviour.

That's David K. Hurst's conclusion too – that 'senior managers aren't cooks, they're ingredients'. But will this keep management on the rails? The next piece tells why British trains today ride on the rails determined by the size of Roman chariots.

So, how to reconcile all this? Easy, according to Richard Pascale's investigation of how Honda really gained such immense success in the American motorcycle business. In effect, the cooks were on the ground, where they learned their way off the old rails. The parable that follows reinforces Pascale's findings. It compares American with Japanese management. Pascale's message is three cheers for middle managers. And next comes more cheers for our worldly, wounded and especially wiki world, which Jonathan Gosling describes in his thoughtful piece.

Henry Mintzberg puts all of 'incrementalism' in perspective with a short piece on 'crafting strategy'. He challenges the popular view of the strategist as someone sitting on a pedestal, dictating brilliant strategies for everyone else to implement, proposing instead a view of the strategist as pattern recogniser, a learner who manages a process in which strategies emerge through all sorts of efforts.

'CHANGE MANAGEMENT' IS AN OXYMORON
BY JIM CLEMMER

A dubious consulting industry and 'profession' has developed, claiming to provide 'change management' services. Those two words make about as much sense together as 'holy war' [and] 'nonworking mother' . . . 'Change management' comes from the same dangerously seductive reasoning as strategic planning. They're both based on the shaky assumption that there's an orderly thinking and implementation process which can objectively plot a course of action, like Jean-Luc Picard on the starship *Enterprise*, and then 'make it so'. But if that ever was possible, it certainly isn't in today's world of high velocity change.

Change can be ignored, resisted, responded to, capitalized upon, and created. But it can't be managed

Change can't be managed. Change can be ignored, resisted, responded to, capitalized upon, and created. But it can't be managed and made to march to some orderly step-by-step process . . . Whether we become change victims or victors depends on our readiness for change . . . [As Abraham Lincoln] once said, 'I will prepare myself and my time must come.' That's how change is managed.

. . . We can't quickly win back customers who've quietly slipped away because of neglect and poor service. We can't suddenly turn our organization into an innovative powerhouse in six months because the market shifted. We can't radically and quickly re-engineer years of sloppy habits and convoluted processes when revolutionary new technology appears. When cost pressures build, we can't dramatically flatten our organizations and suddenly empower everyone who has had years of traditional command and control conditioning. These are long-term culture, system, habit, and skill changes. They need to be improved before they're needed. In the words of an ancient Chinese proverb, 'dig a well before you are thirsty'.

. . . To effectively deal with change you don't focus on change as some kind of manageable force. You deal with change by improving you. And then your time must come . . .

Source: Adapted by Jim Clemmer from Jim Clemmer, *Pathways to Performance*, www.jimclemmer.com, 1995.

SENIOR MANAGERS AREN'T COOKS, THEY'RE INGREDIENTS
BY DAVID K. HURST

In the final analysis, when it comes to fundamental change in organizations, there can be no *final analysis*. For it is the very frameworks of analysis that need to be changed. In fundamental organizational change, *it takes behavior to change behavior: change cannot be managed, it can only be led*. Thus, managers of change are not just cooks preparing a meal by following a recipe, they are also key ingredients. Senior managers are powerful role models, and their key contribution to the process of change is to lead by modeling the new behaviors that they expect of their people. They can plan and orchestrate the arrangements only up to a point. Then they have to throw themselves into the mixture with everyone else and trust that their behavior will be copied by others . . .

Our Western bias is to believe that we can think our way into a better way of *acting*. Experience with real change suggests that just the opposite is true – we have to *act* our way into a better way of *thinking*. As managers, the only behavior we can hope to change directly is our own.

Source: Excerpted from an article originally published as 'When it comes to real change, too much objectivity may be fatal to the process', by David K. Hurst, *Strategy and Leadership*, March/April 1997, pp. 6–12.

STAYING ON TRACK

The U.S. standard railroad gauge (distance between the rails) is 4 feet 8.5 inches. That is an exceedingly odd number. Why was that gauge used? Because that's the way they built them in England, and the U.S. railroads were built by English expatriates. Why did the English build them that way? Because the first rail lines were built by the same people who built the pre-railroad tramways, and that's the gauge they used. Why did 'they' use that gauge? Because the people who built the tramways used the same jigs and tools that they used for building wagons, which used that wheel spacing.

So why did the wagons have that particular odd spacing? Well, if they tried to use any other spacing, the wagon wheels would break on some of the old, long distance roads in England, because that was the spacing of the wheel ruts.

So who built those old rutted roads? The first long distance roads in Europe (and England) were built by Imperial Rome for their legions. The roads have been used ever since. And the ruts in the roads? The ruts in the roads, which everyone had to match for fear of destroying their wagon wheels, were first formed by Roman war chariots. Since the chariots were made for (or by) Imperial Rome, they were all alike in the matter of wheel spacing.

The U.S. standard railroad gauge of 4 feet 8.5 inches derives from the original specification for an Imperial Roman war chariot. Specifications and bureaucracies live forever. So the next time you are handed a specification and wonder what horse's ass came up with it, you may be exactly right, because the Imperial Roman war chariots were made just wide enough to accommodate the back end of two war horses. Thus we have the answer to the original question.

Now for the twist to the story. When we see a space shuttle sitting on its launching pad, there are two booster rockets attached to the side of the main fuel tank. These are solid rocket boosters, or SRBs. The SRBs are made by Thiokol at their factory in Utah. The engineers who designed the SRBs might have preferred to make them a bit fatter, but the SRBs had to be shipped by train from the factory to the launch site. The railroad from the factory had to run through a tunnel in the mountains. The tunnel is slightly wider than the railroad track, and the railroad track is about as wide as two horses' rumps. So, a major design feature of what is arguably the world's most advanced transportation system was determined over two thousand years ago by the width of a horse's ass!

Don't you just love engineering?

Source: Anon.

BACKING INTO A BRILLIANT STRATEGY
BY RICHARD PASCALE

In 1959, Honda, a Japanese manufacturer of motorcycles, not (yet) automobiles, entered the American market. By 1966, it had 63 percent of that market. Partly the company beat American and British manufacturers in selling large motorcycles to what was the initial market: macho, black-leather jacket types. And partly it created a new market for small motorcycles driven by ordinary people, thanks to a legendary advertising campaign called 'You meet the nicest people on a Honda'. The company had in fact been producing these small motorcycles for the Japanese market since the 1940s, when Takeo Fujisawa convinced his partner, Soichiro Honda, whose love was designing and racing big motorcycles, that many of the Japanese people could not afford automobiles post-war but would be amenable to small inexpensive motorcycles for regular transportation.

The British government, whose motorcycle manufacturers saw their share of the import market drop from 49 to 10 percent in that 1959–1966 period, hired the Boston Consulting Group to explain what happened and suggest how their manufacturers could come back. BCG replied, in 1975, in a report that became famous, and formed the basis for cases written at schools such as Harvard and UCLA.

Two excerpts from that report are reproduced below, to give the sense of it. This is followed by the transcript of parts of an interview held by Richard Pascale, co-author of *The Art of Japanese Management* (1981), who had his doubts about the BCG report, with the Honda managers who were responsible for the entry into the American market. The story speaks for itself; so does the contrast between the two interpretations.

Various excerpts related to these two stories are then reproduced.

From the Boston Consulting Group report

The success of the Japanese motorcycle industry originated with the growth of their domestic market during the 1950s. [By 1960] . . . they had developed huge production volumes in small motorcycles in their domestic market, and volume-related cost reductions had followed. This resulted in a highly competitive cost position which the Japanese used as a springboard for penetration of world markets with small motorcycles in the early 1960s . . .

The Japanese motorcycle industry, and in particular Honda, the market leader, present a [consistent] picture. The basic philosophy of the Japanese manufacturer is that high volumes per model provide the potential for high productivity as a result of using capital intensive and highly automated techniques. Their marketing strategies are therefore directed towards developing these high volume models, hence the careful attention that we have observed them giving to growth and market share, and then in production, the cost reduction potential is realized in practice as a result of a primary focus on production engineering and investment for cost reduction.

SOURCE: BOSTON CONSULTING GROUP, *STRATEGY ALTERNATIVES FOR THE BRITISH INDUSTRY*, 1975.

From the interview with the Honda managers

In truth we had no strategy other than the idea of seeing if we could sell something in the United States . . . [We had] to obtain a currency allocation from the Ministry of Finance. They were extraordinarily skeptical. Toyota had launched the Toyopet in the U.S. in 1958 and had failed miserably. 'How could Honda succeed?' they asked. Months went by. We put the project on hold. Suddenly, five months after our application, we were given the go-ahead – but at only a fraction of our expected level of commitment. 'You can invest $250,000 in the U.S. market,' they said, 'but only $110,000 in cash'. The remainder of our assets had to be in parts and motorcycle inventory . . .

Our focus . . . was to compete with the European exports. We knew our products at the time were good but not far superior. Mr. Honda was especially confident of the 250cc and 305cc machines. The shape of the handlebar on these larger machines looked like the eyebrow of Bhudda, which he felt was a strong selling point. Thus, after some discussion and with no compelling criteria for selection, we configured our start-up inventory with 25 percent of each of our four products – the 50cc Supercub, and the 125cc, 250cc and 305cc. In dollar value terms, of course, the inventory was heavily weighted toward the larger bikes.

The stringent monetary controls of the Japanese government together with the unfriendly reception we had received during our 1958 visit caused us to start small. We chose Los Angeles where there was a large second and third generation Japanese community, a climate suitable for motorcycle use, and a growing population. We were so strapped for cash that the three of us shared a furnished apartment that we rented for $80 per month. Two of us slept on the floor. We obtained a warehouse in a run-down section of the city and waited for the ship to arrive. Not daring to spare our funds for equipment, the three of us stacked the motorcycle crates three high – by hand – swept the floors, and built and maintained the parts bin.

We were entirely in the dark the first year. We were not aware that the motorcycle business in the United States occurs during a seasonal April-to-August window – and our timing coincided with the closing of the 1959 season. Our hard-learned experiences with distributorships in Japan convinced us to try to go to the retailers direct. We ran ads in the motorcycle trade magazine for dealers. A few responded. By spring of 1960, we had forty dealers and some of our inventory in their stores – mostly larger bikes. A few of the 250cc and 305cc bikes began to sell. Then disaster struck. By the first week of April 1960, reports were coming in that our machines were leaking oil and encountering clutch failure. This was our lowest moment. Honda's fragile reputation was being destroyed before it could be established. As it turned out, motorcycles in the United States are driven much farther and much faster than in Japan. But not knowing that, we had to dig deeply into our precious cash reserves to air freight our motorcycles to the Honda testing lab in Japan. Throughout the dark month of April, Pan Am was the only enterprise in the U.S. that was nice to us. Our testing lab worked twenty-four-hour days bench testing the bikes to try to replicate the failure. Within a month, a redesigned head gasket and clutch spring solved the problem. But in the meantime, events had taken a surprising turn.

Honda's fragile reputation was being destroyed before it could be established

Throughout our first eight months, following Mr. Honda's and our own instincts, we had not attempted to move the 50cc Supercubs. While they were a smash success in Japan (and manufacturing couldn't keep up with demand there), they seemed wholly unsuitable for the U.S. market where everything was bigger and more luxurious. As a clincher, we had our sights on the import market – and the Europeans, like the American manufacturers, emphasized the larger machines.

We used the Honda 50s ourselves to ride around Los Angeles on errands. They attracted a lot of attention. One day we had a call from a Sears buyer. While persisting in our refusal to sell through an intermediary, we took note of Sears' interest. But we still hesitated to push the 50cc bikes out of fear they might harm our image in a heavily macho market. But when the larger bikes started breaking, we had no choice. We let the 50cc bikes move.

Source: From an article originally entitled 'Perspectives on strategy: the real story behind Honda's success'. Copyright © 1984 by the Regents of the University of California. Reprinted from the *California Management Review*, Vol. 27, No. 1. By permission of the Regents.

A MODERN PARABLE

A Japanese company and an American company decided to have a canoe race on the Missouri River. Both teams practiced long and hard to reach their peak performance before the race.

On the big day, the Japanese won by a mile.

The Americans, very discouraged and depressed, decided to investigate the reason for the crushing defeat. A management team made up of senior management was formed to investigate and recommend appropriate action. Their conclusion was the Japanese had 8 people rowing and 1 person steering, while the American team had 8 people steering and 1 person rowing.

Feeling a deeper study was in order, American management hired a consulting company and paid them a large amount of money for a second opinion. They advised, of course, that too many people were steering the boat, while not enough people were rowing.

Not sure of how to utilize that information, but wanting to prevent another loss to the Japanese, the rowing team's management structure was totally reorganized to 4 steering supervisors, 3 area steering superintendents and 1 assistant superintendent steering manager.

They also implemented a new performance system that would give the 1 person rowing the boat greater incentive to work harder. It was called the 'Rowing Team Quality First Program', with meetings, dinners and free pens for the rower. There was discussion of getting new paddles, canoes and other equipment, extra vacation days for practices and bonuses.

The next year the Japanese won by two miles.

Humiliated, the American management laid off the rower for poor performance, halted development of a new canoe, sold the paddles, and canceled all capital investments for new equipment. The money saved was distributed to the Senior Executives as bonuses and the next year's racing team was out-sourced to India.

Sadly, The End.

Sad, but oh so true! Here's something else to think about: Ford has spent the last thirty years moving all its factories out of the US, claiming they can't make money paying American wages. Toyota has spent the last thirty years building more than a dozen plants inside the US. The last quarter's results: Toyota makes 4 billion in profits while Ford racked up 9 billion in losses. Ford folks are still scratching their heads.

Source: unknown.

WITHER OUR WIKI, WORLDLY, WOUNDED WORLD?
BY JONATHAN GOSLING

What kind of world are we dealing with? Here are three big things to take account of:

1 It's a *wiki* world. In the old days, knowledge was stored up in banks – called schools, colleges and universities, in planning departments and expert systems. University researchers, for example, would go out into the world to gather information, take it back to their labs and libraries, and some years later publish the general rules and patterns. Meanwhile everyone else got on with life. But now, thanks to the internet, anyone can publish the lessons learned from daily work; we can all comment on each others' ideas, and thus knowledge becomes almost immediately actionable. This has a big impact on power – the most important basis of leadership. If leaders no longer control what people know about, they must exert influence by their ability to make connections, to facilitate the actions and opinions of well-informed knowledge-rich active citizens.

2 It's a *worldly* world. We are getting used to seeing how all the parts interconnect: global warming will create vast diasporas of displaced people, so we will all be faced with radical challenges to our shared identity – Who is to say who belongs *here* if we have collectively destroyed *there*? Equally stimulating will be the opportunities offered by a population with family connections all over the world. Previous diasporas have created hugely valuable networks of trusted clan members, but many of them living in ghettoes, taking generations to assimilate and belong in their new-found homes. But with so many more people on the move, how will we sustain communities and shared values and traditions?

Historically, when communities are faced with the twin challenges of asserting a common identity and seizing opportunities for improvement, they have tended to throw up charismatic leaders – and have often resorted to xenophobic scapegoating and military adventure, usually ending badly. Can we prepare and promote a wiser and more caring variety of leader?

3 It's a *wounded* world, socially and environmentally, stuggling to deal with the damage we are doing. This is not all new: in many ways, it's the same old world. Most things continue: we need to eat, preferably with savour;

to educate ourselves and others, enjoy nature, care for the people we love and deepen our humanity through art, culture and spiritual life. Heaven save us from leaders who champion change if they forget or ignore all that continues and should be preserved! This is where distributed leadership becomes crucial; no central authority or charismatic hero can know enough detail about the particular pleasures and local conditions of our lives; it's down to us to get organised (loosely) and vocal (sonorously), and to take a lead in making things better.

save us from leaders who champion change if they forget or ignore all that continues and should be preserved!

Now for 3 small things to develop the leaders and types of leadership that we need:

i The best way to predict who will take initiative and serve as a leader is to see what young people do at school. Participating in sports, school clubs and volunteering in the community are all strongly correlated with activism in later life. Strengthening our youth organisations is a real and proven way of growing leadership for the region. And as many people born and raised here are likely to return in later life, even if they have moved away between, this is a long term investment with several pay-back opportunities.

ii Travel broadens the mind, and there is nothing like it for giving a sense of proportion to incipient grandiosity. Humility – plain realism to most of us – is an unlikely leadership trait, but vital if we are to remain sane and well balanced. The best way to root it to the core of our attitudes is to discover how very peculiar we are – by looking at ourselves through the eyes of others. We should find low-carbon ways to travel, slowly so we can watch and listen, absorbing worldviews and priorities other than our own. This is an investment in tolerance, but also in cultural conviction, knowing what we really treasure. What all this adds up to is that we want leaders who are wise in their judgements about what really matters to us, and are able to adapt and preserve these through the complex changes ahead.

iii If everyone is creating their own version of knowledge, who is to say what's right? I suppose there will still be some use for authorities on arcane subjects – we are bound to need some Professors. But much more significantly, we must ensure that we are all sensing, thinking, feeling, and judging as wisely as possible. We must make ourselves as fully human as we can – not merely rich. As John Ruskin famously said, 'There is no wealth but life',[1] by which he meant a life force, the aspiration to beauty and harmony. We are blessed with wonderful nature and vivid arts here in the South West; we should accept no-one into leadership who is not a lover of the arts; we should train our leaders in culture and creativity – and that means all of us, because in the world of *wikipedia*, we are all authors and authorities.

Ours is indeed a *wiki* world, a worldly world, and in many ways it is a wounded world, in need of care. To produce the wise leaders we need, we should give young people an experience of leadership so they recognise the necessities of collective effort and responsibility; encourage travel and meaningful interaction with people very different to ourselves, so that we come to value our own treasures more realistically; and select only people with a love of beauty and culture to lead our institutions both within and beyond the region.

Readers will have noticed that I am much taken with words beginning with 'w' in this article (though I have desisted from mentioning our weather in the West of England, where I live – warm, windy and wet!). The most important reference in the forgoing is to *wise* leadership, because the main question underlying everything I have said is *'wither the world'?* We seem to be on the edge of crises in both the natural and financial climate, circumstances that all too often prompt calls for strong leadership, the rise of charismatic characters and the appeal of simple solutions. These are good and virtuous things – like most people, I like to be well led; and wise leadership is most likely when we share in its making.

Source: Jonathan Gosling, University of Exeter, 2008.

Footnote

1 The opening passage of *Unto this Last*, the book that inspired Mahatma Gandhi and, subsequently, Martin Luther King.

CRAFTING STRATEGY
BY HENRY MINTZBERG

At work, the potter sits before a lump of clay on the wheel. Her mind is on the clay, but she is also aware of sitting between her past experiences and her future prospects. She knows exactly what has and has not worked for her in the past. She also has an intimate knowledge of her capabilities and her materials. As a craftsperson, she senses rather analyzes things. All this is working in her mind as her hands are working the clay. What emerges on the wheel is likely to be in the tradition of her past work, but she may break away and embark on a new direction. Even so, the past is no less present, projecting itself into the future.

Managers are craftspeople and strategy is their clay. Like the potter, they sit between a past of corporate capabilities and a future of market opportunities. And if they are truly craftspeople, they bring to their work an equally intimate knowledge of the materials at hand. That is the essence of crafting strategy.

The popular view sees the strategist as a planner or as a visionary, someone sitting on a pedestal dictating brilliant strategies for everyone else to implement. While recognizing the importance of thinking ahead and especially of the need for creative vision in this pedantic world, I wish to propose an additional view of the strategist – as a pattern recognizer, a learner if you will – who manages a process in which strategies (and visions) can emerge as well as be deliberately conceived. I also wish to redefine that strategist, to extend that someone into the collective entity made up of the many actors whose interplay speaks an organization's mind. This strategist *finds* strategies no less than creates them.

What does it mean to craft strategy? Let us look at the words associated with craft: dedication, experience, involvement with the material, the personal touch, mastery of detail, a sense of harmony and integration. Managers who craft strategy do not spend much time in executive suites reading reports or industry analyses. They are involved, responsive to their materials, learning about their organizations and industries through personal touch. They appreciate that strategies can *form* without being formulated: they can *emerge* as people, learn their way into new patterns that work.

Managers who craft strategy do not spend much time in executive suites reading reports or industry analyses

Manage stability

Managing strategy is mostly managing stability, not change. Indeed, most of the time senior managers should not be formulating strategy at all; they should be getting on with making their organizations as effective as possible in pursing the strategies they already have. Like distinguished craftsmen, organizations become distinguished because they master the details.

To manage strategy, then, at least in the first instance, is not so much to promote change as to know *when* to do so. Organizations that reassess their strategies continuously are like individuals who reassess their jobs or their marriages continuously – they can drive themselves crazy.

So-called strategic planning must be recognized for what it is: a means, not to create strategy, but to program a strategy already created – to work out its implications formally. This process is essentially analytic in nature, while strategy creation is essentially a process of synthesis. That is why trying to create strategies through formal planning most often leads to extrapolating existing ones or copying those of competitors.

Detect discontinuity

Environments do not change on any regular or orderly basis. And they seldom undergo continuous dramatic change, claims about our 'age of discontinuity' and environmental 'turbulence' notwithstanding. Much of the time, change is minor and even temporary and requires no strategic response. Once in a while there is a truly significant discontinuity or, even less often, a gestalt shift in the environment, where everything important seems to change at once. But these events, while critical, are easy to recognize.

The real challenge in crafting strategy lies in detecting the subtle discontinuities that may undermine a business in the future. And for that, there is no technique, no program, just a sharp mind in touch with the situation. The trick is to manage within a given strategic orientation most of the time yet be able to pick out the occasional discontinuity that really matters.

Note the kind of knowledge involved here: not analytical reports or abstracted facts and figures (although these can certainly help), but personal knowledge, intimate understanding, equivalent to the craftsman's feel for the clay. Facts are available to anyone; this kind of knowledge is not.

Manage patterns

A key to managing strategy is the ability to detect emerging patterns and help them take shape. The job of the senior manager is not just to preconceive strategies but also to recognize the emergence of strategies as new patterns anywhere in the organization and intervene when appropriate.

> *Like weeds that appear unexpectedly in a garden, some emergent strategies may need to be uprooted immediately*

Like weeds that appear unexpectedly in a garden, some emergent strategies may need to be uprooted immediately. But management cannot be too quick to cut off the unexpected, for tomorrow's vision may grow out of today's aberration. (Europeans, after all, enjoy salads made from the leaves of the dandelion, America's most notorious weed.) Thus some patterns are worth watching until their effects have more clearly manifested themselves. Then those that prove useful can be made deliberate and so be incorporated into the formal strategy.

Create a fertile climate

To manage in this context, then, is to create the climate within which a wide variety of strategies can grow. In more complex organizations, this may mean building flexible structures, hiring creative people, defining broad visions, and watching for the patterns that emerge.

Appreciate the past

While strategy is a word that is usually associated with the future, its link to the past is no less central. As Kierkegaard once observed, life is lived forward but understood backward. Managers may have to live strategy in the future, but they must understand it through the past.

Like potters at the wheel, organizations must make sense of the past if they hope to manage the future. Only by coming to understand the patterns that form in their own behavior do they get to know their capabilities and their potential. Thus crafting strategy, like managing craft, requires a natural synthesis of the future, present, and past.

Growing strategic flowers on the ground

Strategies are not tablets conceived atop mountains, to be carried down for execution; they are learned on the ground by anyone who has the experience and capacity to see the general beyond the specifics. Remaining in the stratosphere of the conceptual is no better than having one's feet firmly planted in concrete.

Add all this up and it appears that managers may be most effective as strategists by letting a thousand strategic flowers bloom in their organizational gardens, rather than trying to raise their strategies in a hothouse. Thus, the strategy process is close to craft and enhanced by art. Science enters the process at the beginning and end but not in the middle. In the form of analyses, it feeds in data and findings, and at the end of the process it programs the strategies that come out by other means.

Source: Adapted from an article by this title in the *Harvard Business Review*, September–October, 1987. Copyright © 1987 by the Harvard Business School Publishing Corporation; all rights reserved. See also *Tracking Strategies*, Oxford University Press, 2007, and *Strategy Safari*, Pearson, 1998.

All change seems impossible, but once accomplished, it is the state you are no longer in that seems impossible. Alain

CHAPTER 8
MANAGING MODESTLY

The fox knows many things but the hedgehog knows one big thing. [Achilochas, circa 650 BC]

So – what to do about all this? Well – how about managing more modestly? More thoughtfully, more sensitively, but especially more modestly. People can manage modestly in all kinds of ways, as the readings point out. They can simply come to understand what gets in their way (for example, about being the deputy quartermaster in India, in our first piece); they can refuse obscene pay packages for the sake of teamwork, so that people really can become 'a company's greatest asset' (as in our second piece, a fantasy letter by a CEO to the board); they can let everyone have ideas (our third piece). Overall, they can simply manage quietly. And they can even consider what managing would be like without managers (our last two pieces).

YEE GODS, WHAT DO I DO NOW?
BY IAN HAMILTON

. . . In 1896 I was Deputy Quartermaster-General at Simla; then, perhaps
still, one of the hardest worked billets in Asia. After a long office day I used
to get back home to dinner pursued by a pile of files three to four feet high.
The Quartermaster-General, my boss, was a clever, delightful work-glutton.
So we sweated and ran together for a while a neck and neck race with our
piles of files, but I was the younger and he was the first to be ordered off
by the doctors to Europe. Then I, at the age of forty-three, stepped into the
shoes and became officiating Quartermaster-General in India. Unluckily,
the Government at that moment was in a very stingy mood. They refused
to provide pay to fill the post I was vacating and Sir George White, the
Commander-in-Chief, asked me to duplicate myself and do the double
work. My heart sank, but there was nothing for it but to have a try. The day
came; the Quartermaster-General went home and with him went the whole
of his share of the work. As for my own share, the hard twelve hours' task
melted by some magic into the Socialist's dream of a six hours' day. How
was that? Because, when a question came up from one of the Departments I
had formerly been forced to compose a long minute upon it, explaining the
case, putting my own views, and endeavoring to persuade the Quartermaster-
General to accept them. He was a highly conscientious man and if he differed
from me he liked to put on record his reasons – several pages of reasons.
Or, if he agreed with me, still he liked to agree in his own words and to 'put
them on record'. Now, when I became Quartermaster-General and Deputy-
Quartermaster General rolled into one I studied the case as formerly, but
there my work ended: I had not to persuade my own subordinates: I had no
superior except the Commander-in-Chief, who was delighted to be left alone:
I just gave an order – quite a simple matter unless a man's afraid: 'Yes,' I said,
or 'No!'

Source: Sir Ian Hamilton, *The Soul and Body of an Army*, E. Arnold & Co., 1921, pp. 235–236. © by kind
permission of the Trustees of the Estate of Sir Ian Hamilton.

A LONG OVERDUE LETTER TO THE BOARD
BY HENRY MINTZBERG

Dear Members of the Board

I am writing to you with a proposal that may seem radical. In fact it
is conservative, for my primary role as Chief Executive Officer of this
corporation is to ensure its conservation as a healthy enterprise.

I am requesting that you reduce my salary by half and that you redesign
my bonus system along the lines outlined below. From now on, I wish to

take increases (or decreases for that matter) in the same proportion as our operating employees.

I have talked a great deal about teamwork during my tenure in this job, that we are all in this together, all of our people. Yet I am singled out by virtue of my compensation. How can I foster real teamwork when a disproportionate share of the benefits comes to me? (Lately, as more and more of our people become aware of my compensation, I have been getting increasing amounts of hate mail about it. This is certainly disconcerting, but most troublesome is that I have no reasonable reply to it.)

How can I foster real teamwork when a disproportionate share of the benefits comes to me?

The assumption these days seems to be that the CEO does it all. I certainly lead, but only by respecting the contribution made by others.

My job is to release the energy that exists within our people. What makes true that old adage about leadership – that people will say they did it themselves – is that they really do. Real leaders know that. CEOs who have to fix everything are all too often succeeded by organizations that collapse. We will all have been successful if this place is as profitable after I am gone as it is now.

And that brings me to my second point. We talk a lot in our meetings about the long term health of this company. Well then, why then am I being rewarded for short term gains in the stock price? And why always those narrow numbers? We all know that I have all sorts of ways to cut spending at the expense of our future. If you want to reward me on the basis of those numbers, then save it – until five years after I retire. Then you'll know!

Ever since we started this shareholder value business, our culture has gone to hell. Our frontline employees tell me it gets in the way of serving customers: they are forced to see dollar signs out there, not real people. And more and more of them just don't give a damn any more: we don't count, they tell me, so why should we care. All of us shall pay dearly for these short term gains, I assure you. In fact, I wonder if this productivity surge being experienced in America is nothing more than the gains from short term cost cutting – at the expense of real productivity. After all, it doesn't take geniuses to close things and cut things. Building things is the hard part; are we doing enough of that?

It doesn't take geniuses to close things and cut things

I have always prided myself on being a risk taker. That is one of the reasons you put me in this job. So let's take a look at my compensation scheme. I cash in big time when the stock goes up, but pay out nothing when the stock goes down. I don't even have to give back a penny of what I gained last year if the price turns around and drops this year. Some risk taker! You know what: I'm tired of being a hypocrite.

And why just me? Why not all of us equally? I propose that I receive no higher bonus, in proportion to my salary, than anyone else in this company. We claim to be a sophisticated 'network' of 'knowledge workers' marching into the third millennium. Isn't it time we brought our practices in line with our rhetoric?

Now I know the line we have been using all along: that I am only being compensated to keep up with others in my position. Enough of this complicity in behavior we all know to be outrageous. Frankly, I don't care if his is bigger than mine. My salary should not be some kind of external trophy. It is above all an internal signal, to tell our people what we really think about this place. Let's stop pretending that CEOs form some kind of elite club. It is leadership we are talking about here, not status.

To be perfectly honest, I am so busy running this company that I hardly have the time to spend all this money I make, let alone to so with a conspicuousness that demonstrates how much it is. My family and I are well looked after, I assure you, even at the income level I propose. Let me concentrate on trying to manage this place as it should be managed.

I trust you have read this letter as an investment in our future. Because if our company has no future in these terms, then neither does our society.

Sincerely,

Chief Executive Officer

Source: Henry Mintzberg 'There's no compensation for hypocrisy', Financial Times, October 29 1999.

HERE'S AN IDEA: LET EVERYONE HAVE IDEAS
BY WILLIAM C. TAYLOR

Like many top executives, James R. Lavoie and Joseph M. Marino keep a close eye on the stock market. But the two men, co-founders of Rite-Solutions, a software company that builds advanced – and highly classified – command-and-control systems for the Navy, don't worry much about Nasdaq or the New York Stock Exchange.

Instead, they focus on an internal market where any employee can propose that the company acquire a new technology, enter a new business or make an efficiency improvement. These proposals become stocks, complete with ticker symbols, discussion lists and e-mail alerts. Employees buy or sell the stocks, and prices change to reflect the sentiments of the company's engineers, computer scientists and project managers – as well as its marketers, accountants and even the receptionist.

'We're the founders, but we're far from the smartest people here,' Mr. Lavoie, the chief executive, said during an interview at Rite-Solutions' headquarters outside Newport, R.I. 'At most companies, especially technology companies, the most brilliant insights tend to come from people other than senior management. So we created a marketplace to harvest collective genius.'

That's a refreshing dose of humility from a successful C.E.O. with decades of experience in his field. (Mr. Lavoie, 59, is a Vietnam War veteran and an accomplished engineer who has devoted his career to military-oriented technologies.)

Most companies operate under the assumption that big ideas come from a few big brains: the inspired founder, the eccentric inventor, the visionary boss. But there's a fine line between individual genius and know-it-all arrogance. What happens when rivals become so numerous, when technologies move so quickly, that no corporate honcho can think of everything? Then it's time to invent a less top-down approach to innovation, to make it everybody's business to come up with great ideas.

That's a key lesson behind the rise of open source technology, most notably Linux. A ragtag army of programmers organized into groups, wrote computer code, made the code available for anyone to revise and, by competing and cooperating in a global community, reshaped the market for software. The brilliance of Linux as a model of innovation is that it is powered by the grass-roots brilliance of the thousands of programmers who created it.

It's time to invent a less top-down approach to innovation, to make it everybody's business to come up with great ideas.

According to Tim O'Reilly, the founder and chief executive of O'Reilly Media, the computer book publisher, and an evangelist for open source technologies, creativity is no longer about which companies have the most visionary executives, but who has the most compelling 'architecture of participation'. That is, which companies make it easy, interesting and rewarding for a wide range of contributors to offer ideas, solve problems and improve products?

At Rite-Solutions, the architecture of participation is both businesslike and playful. Fifty-five stocks are listed on the company's internal market, which is called Mutual Fun. Each stock comes with a detailed description – called an expect-us, as opposed to a prospectus – and begins trading at a price of $10. Every employee gets $10,000 in 'opinion money' to allocate among the offerings, and employees signal their enthusiasm by investing in a stock and, better yet, volunteering to work on the project. Volunteers share in the proceeds, in the form of real money, if the stock becomes a product or delivers savings.

Mr. Marino, 57, president of Rite-Solutions, says the market, which began in January 2005, has already paid big dividends. One of the earliest stocks was a proposal to apply three-dimensional visualization technology, akin to video games, to help sailors and domestic-security personnel practice making decisions in emergency situations. Initially, Mr. Marino was unenthusiastic about the idea – 'I'm not a joystick jockey' – but support among employees was overwhelming. Today, that product line, called Rite-View, accounts for 30 percent of total sales.

'Would this have happened if it were just up to the guys at the top?' Mr. Marino asked. 'Absolutely not. But we could not ignore the fact that so many people were rallying around the idea. This system removes the terrible burden of us always having to be right.'

Another virtue of the stock market, Mr. Lavoie added, is that it finds good ideas from unlikely sources. Among Rite-Solutions' core technologies are pattern-recognition algorithms used in military applications, as well as for electronic gambling systems at casinos, a big market for the company. A member of the administrative staff, with no technical expertise, thought that this technology might also be used in educational settings, to create an entertaining way for students to learn history or math.

She started a stock called Win/Play/Learn, which attracted a rush of investment from engineers eager to turn her idea into a product. Their enthusiasm led to meetings with Hasbro, up the road in Pawtucket, and Rite-Solutions won a contract to help it build its VuGo multimedia system, introduced last Christmas.

Mr. Lavoie called this innovation an example of the 'quiet genius' that goes untapped inside most organizations. 'We would have never connected those dots,' he said. 'But one employee floated an idea, lots of employees got passionate about it and that led to a new line of business.'

...an example of the 'quiet genius' that goes untapped inside most organizations

The next frontier is to tap the quiet genius that exists outside organizations – to attract innovations from people who are prepared to work with a company, even if they don't work for it. An intriguing case in point is InnoCentive, a virtual research and development lab through which major corporations invite scientists and engineers worldwide to contribute ideas and solve problems they haven't been able to crack themselves.

InnoCentive, based in Andover, Mass., is literally a marketplace of ideas. It has signed up more than 30 blue-chip companies, including Procter & Gamble, Boeing and DuPont, whose research labs are groaning under the weight of unsolved problems and unfinished projects. It has also signed up more than 90,000 biologists, chemists and other professionals from more than 175 countries. These 'solvers' compete to meet thorny technical challenges posted by 'seeker' companies. Each challenge has a detailed scientific description, a deadline and an award, which can run as high as $100,000.

'We are talking about the democratization of science,' said Alpheus Bingham, who spent 28 years as a scientist and senior research executive at Eli Lilly & Company before becoming the president and chief executive of InnoCentive. 'What happens when you open your company to thousands and thousands of minds, each of them with a totally different set of life experiences?'

InnoCentive, founded as an independent start-up by Lilly in 2001, has an impressive record. It can point to a long list of valuable scientific ideas that have arrived, with surprising speed, from faraway places. In addition to the United States, the top countries for solvers are China, India and Russia.

Last month, InnoCentive attracted a $9 million infusion of venture capital to accelerate its growth. 'There is a "collective mind" out there,' Dr. Bingham said. 'The question for companies is, what fraction of it can you access?'

That remains an unanswered question at many companies, whose leaders continue to rely on their own brainpower as the key source of ideas. But there's evidence that more and more top executives are recognizing the limits of their individual genius.

Back at Rite-Solutions, for example, one of the most valuable stocks on Mutual Fun is the stock market itself. So many executives from other companies have asked to study the system that a team championed the idea of licensing it as a product – another unexpected opportunity.

'There's nothing wrong with experience,' said Mr. Marino, the company's president. 'The problem is when experience gets in the way of innovation. As founders, the one thing we know is that we don't know all the answers.'

MANAGING QUIETLY
BY HENRY MINTZBERG

A prominent business magazine hires a journalist to write about the chief executive of a major corporation. The man has been at the helm for several years and is considered highly effective. The journalist submits an excellent piece, capturing the very spirit of the man's managerial style. The magazine rejects it – not exciting enough, no hype. Yet the company has just broken profit records for its industry.

Not far away, another major corporation is undergoing dramatic transformation. Change is everywhere, the place is teeming with consultants, people are being released in huge numbers. The chief executive has been all over the business press. Suddenly he is fired: the board considers the turnaround a failure.

Go back five, ten, twenty or more years and read the business press – about John Scully at Apple, James Robinson at American Express, Robert McNamara at the Defense Department. Heroes of American management all . . . for a time. Then consider this proposition: maybe really good management is boring. Maybe the press is the problem, alongside the so-called gurus, since they are the ones who personalize success and deify the leaders (before they defile them). After all, corporations are large and complicated; it takes a lot of effort to find out what has really been going on. It is much easier to assume that the great one did it all. Makes for better stories.

If you want to test this proposition, try Switzerland. It is a well-run country. No arounds. Ask the next Swiss you meet the name of the head of state. Don't be surprised she does not know: the seven people who run the country sit around a table, rotating position on an annual basis . . .

The problem is the present

. . . *Today, today,* always *today.* This is the voice of the obsessively analytic mind, shouting into today's wind.

But if you want the imagination to see the future, then you'd better have the wisdom to appreciate the past. An obsession with the present – with what's 'hot' and what's 'in' – may be dazzling, but all that does is blind everyone to the reality. Show me a chief executive who ignores yesterday, who favors the new outsider over the experienced insider, the quick fix over steady progress, and I'll show you a chief executive who is destroying an organization.

To 'turn around' is to end up facing the same way. Maybe that is the problem: all this turning around. Might not the white knight of management be the black hole of organizations? What good is the great leader if everything collapses when he or she leaves? Perhaps good companies don't need to be turned around at all because they are not constantly being thrust into crises by leaders who have to make their marks today. Maybe these companies are simply managed quietly.

Managing quietly

What has been the greatest advance ever in health care? Not the dramatic discoveries of penicillin or insulin, it has been argued, but simply cleaning up the water supply. Perhaps, then, it is time to clean up our organizations, as well as our thinking. In this spirit I offer a few thoughts about some of the quiet words of managing.

● *Inspiring:* Quiet managers don't empower their people – 'empowerment' is taken for granted. They *inspire* them. They create the conditions that foster openness and release energy. The queen bee, for example, does not make decisions; she just emits a chemical substance that holds the whole social system together. In human hives, that is called *culture*.

Quiet managers strengthen the cultural bonds between people, not by treating them as detachable 'human resources' (probably the most offensive term ever coined in management, at least until 'human capital' came along), but as respected members of a cohesive social system. When people are trusted, they do not have to be empowered.

The queen bee does not take credit for the worker bees' doing their jobs effectively. She just does her job effectively, so that they can do theirs. There are no bonuses for the queen bee beyond what she needs.

Next time you hear a chief executive go on about teamwork, about how 'we' did it by all pulling together, ask who among the 'we' is getting what kind of bonus. When you hear that chief boasting about taking the long view, ask how those bonuses are calculated. If cooperation and foresight are so important, why have these few been cashing in on generous stock options? Do we take the money back when the price plummets? Isn't it time to recognize this kind of executive compensation for what it is: a form of corruption, not only of our institutions, but of our societies as democratic systems?

- *Caring:* Quiet managers care for their organizations; they do not try to slice away problems as surgeons do. They spend more time preventing problems than fixing them, because they know enough to know when and how to intervene. In a sense, this is more like homeopathic medicine: the prescription of small doses to stimulate the system to fix itself. Better still, it is like the best of nursing: gentle care that, in itself, becomes cure.

Quiet managers spend more time preventing problems than fixing them

- *Infusing:* 'If you want to know what problems we have encountered over the years,' someone from a major airline once told me, 'just look at our headquarters units. Every time we have a problem, we create a new unit to deal with it.' That is management by intrusion. Stick in someone or something to fix it. Ignore everyone and everything else: that is the past. What can the newly arrived chief know about the past, anyway? Besides, the stock analysts and magazine reporters don't have the time to allow the new chief to find out.

  Quiet managing is about *infusion*, change that seeps in slowly, steadily, profoundly. Rather than having change thrust upon them in dramatic, superficial episodes, everyone takes responsibility for making sure that serious changes take hold.

  This does not mean changing everything all the time – which is just another way of saying anarchy. It means always changing some things while holding most others steady. Call this *natural* continuous improvement, if you like. The trick, of course, is to know what to change when. And to achieve that there is no substitute for a leadership with an intimate understanding of the organization working with a workforce that is respected and trusted. That way, when people leave, including the leaders, progress continues.

- *Initiating:* Moses supplies our image of the strategy process: walking down the mountain carrying the word from on high to the waiting faithful. Redemption from the heavens. Of course, there are too many people to read the tablets, so the leaders have to shout these 'formulations' to all these 'implementors'. All so very neat.

  Except that life in the valleys below is rich and complicated. And that is what strategy has to be about – not the neat abstractions of the executive suite, but the messy patterns of daily life. So long as loud management stays up there disconnected, it can shout down all the strategies it likes: they will never work.

  Quiet management is . . . about rolling up sleeves and finding out what is going on. And it is not parachuted down on the organization; it rises up from the base. But it never leaves that base. It functions 'on the floor', where the knowledge for strategy making lies. Such management blends into the daily life of the corporation, so that all sorts of people with their feet planted firmly on the ground can pursue exciting initiatives. Then managers who are in touch with them can champion these initiatives and so stimulate the process by which strategies evolve.

  Put differently, the manager is not the organization any more than [a painting of a pipe is a pipe] . . . A healthy organization does not have to leap from one hero to another; it is a collective social system that naturally survives changes in leadership. If you want to judge the leader, look at the organization ten years later.

Beyond quiet

Quiet management is about thoughtfulness rooted in experience. Words like wisdom, trust, dedication, and judgment apply. Leadership works because it is legitimate, meaning that it is an integral part of the organization and so has the respect of everyone there. Tomorrow is appreciated because yesterday is honored. That makes today a pleasure.

Indeed, the best managing of all may well be silent. That way people can say, 'We did it ourselves.' Because we did.

Source: Reprinted with deletions from Henry Mintzberg, 'Managing quietly', *Leader to Leader*, Spring 1999, 24–30.

MANAGING WITHOUT MANAGERS
BY RICARDO SEMLER

In Brazil, where paternalism and the family business fiefdom still flourish, I am president of a manufacturing company that treats its 800 employees like responsible adults. Most of them – including factory workers – set their own working hours. All have access to the company books. The vast majority vote on many important corporate decisions. Everyone gets paid by the month, regardless of job description, and more than 150 of our management people set their own salaries and bonuses . . .

It's never easy to transplant management programs from one company to another. In South America, it's axiomatic that our structure and style cannot be duplicated. Semco is either too small, too big, too far away, too young, too old, or too obnoxious.

We may also be too specialized. We do cellular manufacturing of technologically sophisticated products, and we work at the high end on quality and price . . . Still the merit of sharing experience is to encourage experiment and to plant the seeds of conceptual change . . .

Participatory hot air

The first of Semco's three values is democracy, or employee involvement. Clearly, workers who control their working conditions are going to be happier than workers who don't. Just as clearly, there is no contest between the company that buys the grudging compliance of its work force and the company that enjoys the enterprising participation of its employees.

But about 90% of the time, participatory management is just hot air. Not that intentions aren't good. It's just that implementing employee involvement is so complex, so difficult, and, not uncommonly, so frustrating that it is easier to talk about than to do . . .

The organizational pyramid is the cause of much corporate evil because the tip is too far from the base

Size reduction is essential for putting employees in touch with one another so they can coordinate their work. The kind of distance we want to eliminate comes from having too many people in one place, but it also comes from having a pyramidal hierarchy.

Pyramids and circles

The organizational pyramid is the cause of much corporate evil because the tip is too far from the base. Pyramids emphasize power, promote insecurity, distort communications, hobble interaction, and make it very difficult for the people who plan and the people who execute to move in the same direction. So Semco designed an organizational *circle*. Its greatest advantage is to reduce management levels to three – one corporate level and two operating levels at the manufacturing units.

It consists of three concentric circles. One tiny, central circle contains the five people who integrate the company's movements. These are the counselors I mentioned before. I'm one of them, and except for a couple of legal documents that call me president, counselor is the only title I use. A second, larger circle contains the heads of the eight divisions – we call them partners. Finally, a third, huge circle holds all the other employees. Most of them are the people we call associates; they do the research, design, sales, and manufacturing work and have no one reporting to them on a regular basis. But some of them are the permanent and temporary team and task leaders we call coordinators. We have counselors, partners, coordinators, and associates. That's four titles and three management layers.

The linchpins of the system are the coordinators, a group that includes everyone formerly called foreman, supervisor, manager, head, or chief. The only people who report to coordinators are associates. No coordinator reports to another coordinator – that feature of the system is what ensures the reduction in management layers . . .

Associates often make higher salaries than coordinators and partners, and they can increase their status and compensation without entering the 'management' line.

Managers and the status and money they enjoy – in a word, hierarchy – are the single biggest obstacle to participatory management. We had to get the managers out of the way of democratic decision making, and our circular system does that pretty well.

But we go further. We don't hire or promote people until they've been interviewed and accepted by all their future subordinates. Twice a year, subordinates evaluate managers. Also twice a year, everyone in the company anonymously fills out a questionnaire about company credibility and top management competence. Among other things, we ask our employees what it would take to make them quit or go on strike.

We insist on making important decisions collegially, and certain decisions are made by a company-wide vote. Several years ago, for example, we needed a bigger plant for our marine division, which makes pumps, compressors, and ship propellers. Real estate agents looked for months and found nothing. So we asked the employees themselves to help, and over the first weekend they found three factories for sale, all of them nearby. We closed up shop for a day, piled everyone into buses, and drove out to inspect the three buildings. Then the workers voted – and they chose a plant the counselors didn't really want. It was an interesting situation – one that tested our commitment to participatory management . . .

Employees also outvoted me on the acquisition of a company that I'm still sure we should have bought. But they felt we weren't ready to digest it, and I lost the vote. In a case like that, the credibility of our management system is at stake. Employee involvement must be real, even when it makes management uneasy. Anyway, what is the future of an acquisition if the people who have to operate it don't believe it's workable?

Hiring adults

We have other ways of combating hierarchy too. Most of our programs are based on the notion of giving employees control over their own lives. In a word, we hire adults, and then we treat them like adults.

Think about that. Outside the factory, workers are men and women who elect governments, serve in the army, lead community projects, raise and educate families, and make decisions every day about the future. Friends solicit their advice. Salespeople court them. Children and grandchildren look up to them for their wisdom and experience. But the moment they walk into the factory, the company transforms them into adolescents. They have to wear badges and name tags, arrive at a certain time, stand in line to punch the clock . . .

One of my first moves when I took control of Semco was to abolish norms, manuals, rules, and regulations. Everyone knows you can't run a large organization without regulations, but everyone also knows that most regulations are poppycock. They rarely solve problems . . .

It's also true that common sense requires just a touch of civil disobedience every time someone calls attention to something that's not working . . . so we replaced all the nitpicking regulations with the rule of common sense and put our employees in the demanding position of using their own judgment.

We have no dress code, for example. The idea that personal appearance is important in a job – any job – is baloney . . . A company that needs business suits to prove its seriousness probably lacks more meaningful proof . . . women and men look best when they feel good . . .

We encourage – we practically insist on – job rotation every two to five years to prevent boredom. We try hard to provide job security, and for people over 50 or who've been with the company for more than three years, dismissal procedures are extra complicated.

On the more experimental side, we have a program for entry-level management trainees called Lost in Space, whereby we hire a couple of people every year who have no job description at all. A 'godfather' looks after them, and for one year they can do anything they like, as long as they try at least 12 different areas or units.

By the same logic that governs our other employee programs, we also have eliminated time clocks. People come and go according to their own schedules . . . one man wanted to start at 7 A.M., but because the forklift operator didn't come until 8, he couldn't get his parts. So a general discussion arose, and the upshot was that now everyone knows how to operate a forklift . . .

Hunting the woolly mammoth

. . . As Antony Jay points out, corporate man is a very recent animal. At Semco, we try to respect the hunter that dominated the first 99.9% of the history of our species. If you had to kill a mammoth or do without supper, there was no time to draw up an organization chart, assign tasks, or delegate authority . . .

Put ten people together, don't appoint a leader, and you can be sure that one will emerge. So will a sighter, a runner, and whatever else the group needs. We form the groups, but they find their own leaders. That's not a lack of structure, that's just a lack of structure imposed from above.

But getting back to that mammoth, why was it that all the members of the group were so eager to do their share of the work – sighting, running, spearing, chiefing – and to stand aside when someone else could do it better? Because they all got to eat the thing once it was killed and cooked. What mattered was results, not status.

Corporate profit is today's mammoth meat. And though there is a widespread view that profit sharing is some kind of socialist infection, it seems to me that few motivational tools are more capitalist. Everyone agrees that profits should belong to those who risk their capital, that entrepreneurial behavior deserves reward, that the creation of wealth should enrich the creator. Well, depending on how you define capital and risk, all these truisms can apply as much to workers as to shareholders . . .

Semco's experience has convinced me that profit sharing has an excellent chance of working when it crowns a broad program of employee participation, when the profit-sharing criteria are so clear and simple that the least-gifted employee can understand them, and perhaps most important, when employees have monthly access to the company's vital statistics – costs, overhead, sales, payroll, taxes, profits.

Transparency

. . . Nothing matters more than those vital statistics – short, frank, frequent reports on how the company is doing. Complete transparency. No hocus-pocus, no hanky-panky, no simplifications.

On the contrary, all Semco employees attend classes to learn how to read and understand the numbers, and it's one of their unions that teaches the course. Every month, each employee gets a balance sheet, a profit-and-loss analysis, and a cash-flow statement for his or her division . . .

What matters in budgets as well as in reports is that the numbers be few and important and that people treat them with something approaching passion. The three monthly reports, with their 70 line items, tell us how to run the company, tell our managers how well they know their units, and tell our employees if there's going to be a profit. Everyone works on the basis of the same information, and everyone looks forward to its appearance with what I'd call fervent curiosity.

And that's all there is to it. Participation gives people control of their work, profit sharing gives them a reason to do it better, information tells them what's working and what isn't.

Letting them do whatever the hell they want

So we don't have systems or staff functions or analysts or anything like that. What we have are people who either sell or make, and there's nothing in between. Is there a marketing department? Not on your life. Marketing is everybody's problem. Everybody knows the price of the products. Everybody knows the cost. Everybody has the monthly statement that says exactly what each of them makes, how much bronze is costing us, how much overtime we paid, all of it. And the employees know that 23% of the after-tax profit is theirs.

We are very, very rigorous about the numbers. We want them in on the fourth day of the month so we can get them back out on the fifth. And because we're so strict with the financial controls, we can be extremely lax about everything else. Employees can paint the walls any color they like. They can come to work whenever they decide. They can wear whatever clothing makes them comfortable. They can do whatever the hell they want. It's up to them to see the connection between productivity and profit and to act on it.

Source: Excerpts from Ricardo Semler, 'Managing without managers', *Harvard Business Review*, September–October, 1989. Reprinted by permission of *Harvard Business Review*. Copyright © 1989 by the Harvard Business School Publishing Corporation; all rights reserved.

After all is said and done, more is said than done. Aesop quotes, 620–560 BC

INDEX